Brand Up

The Ultimate Playbook
for College & Career Success
in the Digital World

Stacey Ross Cohen

Praise for *Brand Up*

"If you want to succeed in today's competitive world, then a strong personal brand is an absolute must. That's where Brand Up comes in. Stacey Cohen distills her decades of experience into a step-by-step guide for achieving college and career success. If you want to excel at networking and entrepreneurship in the classroom and in the boardroom, don't miss Brand Up!"

– Barbara Corcoran
Author, ABC's Shark Tank Investor & Speaker

"Like it or not, you will be judged. This book helps you choose from a variety of ways to be sure that you'll be seen the way you want to be seen."
– Seth Godin, Author,
This Is Marketing

"Whether you're working on college admissions, getting a job, moving into the world of trade or entrepreneurship, or chasing your greatest aspirations, Brand Up is a great guide to help build your personal brand and get an edge over your competition."

– David Meltzer, Co-Founder of Sports 1 Marketing,
Bestselling Author and Top Business Coach

"For our under-resourced students, uncertainty for their college and career readiness impedes their future potential. Brand Up provides a step-by-step methodology to tell their stories in a positive, uplifting manner and to empower them to a better future. This book should be in every high school."

– Marc Steren, Co-Founder and Co-CEO, University Startups

"The pandemic has changed the way we work forever. With the rise of technology and the gig economy, it's more important than ever to prepare kids for the future. That's where Brand Up comes in. The book provides students with skills to achieve academic and career success, including goal-setting, building a strong online presence, interviewing, networking, entrepreneurship, and so much more."

– Harry Moseley, former Global Chief Information Officer, Zoom Video Communications

"As a fellow branding expert, as well as an educator and parent of two teenagers, this book could not have come at a more opportune moment. I teach clients and graduate students how crucial it is to define your brand, highlight your superpowers, and differentiate yourself, so you can authentically be YOU. Brand Up champions these very notions! Brand Up instructs and guides our teens and young adults in the importance of thinking strategically while proudly leveraging their skills and unique qualities that make them marketable and successful."

– Allison Kluger, Lecturer at Stanford Graduate School of Business/Communications and Media Coach

"Brand Up is an essential guide for any teen who wants to be successful in life. It is clear, relatable, and most importantly, it prepares teens to thrive in the real world. The self-awareness exercises included throughout the book provide an excellent opportunity for readers to reflect on their beliefs and start making positive changes in their thinking. As a mindset coach, I can attest to the power of having a growth mindset in achieving all kinds of goals — not just those that involve college."

– Natasha Graziano, Mindset coach, Bestselling Author, *Be It Until You Become It***, and Top Motivational Speaker**

"Brand Up is aligned with our mission to inspire current and future generations of women leaders to start and grow their businesses. Empowering youth with entrepreneurial skills will help more women launch their own businesses, creating a more diverse and innovative workforce. We need more women leaders in the world, and this playbook is a significant step toward making that happen."

– Stephanie Cartin, CEO, Entreprenista Media

"Essential life skills often not taught in schools. It's only a matter of time before you will be Googled. High school students, college students, adults. It's inevitable. This easy-to-read workbook provides actionable strategies to help students learn how to effectively tell their personal story and control their own narrative. These essential skills will help give them an edge in all stages of life. An absolute must read."

- Tanya Avrith, M.A. EdTech, Education Strategist, Co- Author, *The Google Infused Classroom*

"To succeed in the modern entrepreneurial age, you NEED to know who you are, showcase your strengths, and authentically tell your story. Brand Up provides valuable insider secrets and tools to help you stand out in a world filled with noise and everyone vying for attention. The personal branding and life skill lessons I gained were essential to my development as a digital entrepreneur."

– KAYKO, Nashville Artist & Songwriter

"*Brand Up* is a game changer. It shows teens how to create a brand that will make them stand out from the crowd and get noticed by colleges, employers, coaches, and more. It also provides tools they need to level up essential life skills such as networking and interviewing."

- Julie Cottineau, Founder & CEO, BrandTwist

"We all need to be aware of how we are presenting ourselves to the world, and teens must be intentional about building a positive digital footprint. Whether seeking to go to college, become an influencer, score a dream internship, or start a business, this playbook will get you started on your journey to success. Packed with tips, tricks, and strategies, Brand Up is a must-read for any teen who wants to get ahead in today's competitive world."

- Courtney Spritzer, CEO, Socialfly

"This is the book I wish I had growing up and the one I want for my children! Drawing on her unparalleled experiences and insights, Stacey Ross Cohen provides so much more than great advice... she offers a practical, accessible, and empowering 'how to' for teens to both imagine and shape their own futures. Brand Up is the ultimate roadmap to flourish in a world of ever-growing complexity and uncertainty."

- Craig Vezina, Co-Founder, CEO, The Spaceship Academy

"Stacey Ross Cohen is an authority on branding! Learning about personal branding is crucial for entrepreneurs of all ages. The sooner you learn it, the better. Brand Up capitalizes on this concept by focusing on teaching teens the value of branding. A perfect subject to learn for the right age group."

– Dr. Anthony M. Criniti IV (aka "Dr. Finance®"), The World's Leading Financial Scientist and Author of three #1 International Bestselling Finance Books

"Take it from me – don't judge personal branding until you've learned about it and have read this book! Although skeptical when I was required to take a personal branding class in high school (taught by contributor Jason Shaffer), this class was life-changing: it helped me become more self-aware, build a solid online reputation, get accepted into my top choice school, and recently nabbed my dream job. As an artistic person and visual learner, I loved being able to create my 'digital footprint' the way I wanted others to see it. Whether applying for a job or college, this book will help you tell your story, find your strengths, and showcase your skills."

- Samantha Hreschak, BFA, University of Central Florida, 2022; Costuming Cast Member, Walt Disney World

"As an educator and a parent, I'm truly grateful for the actionable tools and strategies provided in this engaging book! It isn't easy making something complex and nuanced this accessible, but Stacey Ross Cohen does this masterfully. An essential read for teens, parents, educators, those who influence our future leaders, and really anyone who wants to untap their limitless potential!"

– Lainie Rowell, Bestselling Author, Award-Winning Educator, and TEDx Speaker

"Colleges should produce well-rounded professionals who, not only receive an education, but have also been taught how to understand life. Consequently, being college-ready is also about having life skills. And that is precisely what sets this book apart! More than ever, kids need to develop skills such as personal branding, networking, and interviewing. It's not just about having perfect GPAs and test scores. Plus, it's essential for teens to get a jump start building a positive online presence."

– Anthony R. Davidson, PhD, MBA; Dean, Fordham University, School of Professional and Continuing Studies

A POST HILL PRESS BOOK
ISBN: 978-1-63758-538-2

Brand Up

The Ultimate Playbook for College & Career Success in the Digital World

Cover and book design by Cecile Rothschild

Post Hill Press
New York • Nashville
posthillpress.com

Published in the United States of America
1 2 3 4 5 6 7 8 9 10

ACKNOWLEDGMENTS

am forever grateful for the support of so many on my journey writing this book. You were there when I needed to vent about writer's block or celebrate a breakthrough. You have all made the book — and me — infinitely better.

First and foremost, I want to thank my husband, Bruce, and two daughters, Kelsey and Amanda. They've been my biggest cheerleaders throughout this entire process and were always there for me through countless drafts and revisions, offering love and encouragement at every step. I couldn't love you more!

Thank you to David Bernstein, Aleigha Kely, and the team at Post Hill Press for bringing this book to life. Your unwavering support and belief in me from the very beginning means everything to me.

I'm incredibly grateful and fortunate to collaborate with my colleagues and contributing authors, Jason Shaffer and Alan Katzman, giants in digital leadership, college admissions, and entrepreneurship. Their insights and expertise have been invaluable. I attribute our collaboration directly to Arianna Huffington, who invited me to contribute to the Huffington Post, where I then crossed paths with Jason and Alan after writing a blog. So thank you, Arianna, for your support and inspiration. If it weren't for you, I never would have had the chance to work with Jason and Alan, and the book would not be what it is today.

Thank you, Kevin Zawacki — my editor extraordinaire — for being there through the many iterations of the book and shaping it into what it is today. You have gone above and beyond and I could not have done it without you. Your partnership in this journey means the world to me! And to my dearest Cecile Rothschild whose creative genius and stunning illustrations make the words pop off the page. I consider myself blessed to work with such super talents as Cecile and Kevin.

And a big shout-out to the countless experts — college admissions officers, entrepreneurs, educational consultants, psychologists, recruiters, and of course, students with stellar brands — who supported me and generously shared their knowledge.

I'm forever grateful to a beautiful soul and literary agent, Devra Jacobs, who took a chance on me and pushed me to dig deeper and find my life purpose and the heartbeat of "Brand Up." I also want to shout out to my work family at Co-Communications — especially Jess, my business partner (the Thelma to my Louise), who always has my back and knows me so well she can finish my sentences.

And the many others who have been a big part of my getting there: my twin sister and inspiration Shari Altarac, Dr. and Master Sha, Jennifer Schwabinger, David Hoffman, Sandy Wollman, Jonathan Gravenor, Mindy Hermann, Marty Jeffcock, Henry DeVries, Shannon Malkin Daniels, Diane Silver, Jeanne Stafford, and David Meerman Scott.

Last but not least, I want to thank my mother, Faith, for always having faith in my entrepreneurial spirit, even when I was just 14-years-old and starting my first business. She has been one of my biggest supporters, and inspirations, and is the wind beneath my wings and "can do" attitude.

And finally, I want to acknowledge my readers. I wrote this book for you to bring out your inner champion. Regardless of your path in life, you will learn how to share your unique talents and perspective with the world. I can't wait to see what you achieve!

Thank you all from the bottom of my heart.

Brand Up

SECTION A: DISCOVERY

PART I - WHO ARE YOU ANYWAY?

CONTENTS

PART II – THE FUTURE YOU

SECTION B: DEVELOPMENT

PART III – STAYING ON MESSAGE

PART IV – YOUR PERSONAL BRANDING TOOLKIT

PART V – BUILDING YOUR DIGITAL PORTFOLIO ON LINKEDIN

SECTION C: DELIVERY

PART VI – MANAGING YOUR SOCIAL MEDIA PRESENCE

PART VII – NETWORKING FOR SUCCESS

PROLOGUE

Dear Reader,

Welcome to *Brand Up: The Ultimate Playbook for College & Career Success in the Digital World.* This playbook will equip you with strategies, tools, and exercises to uncover your strengths and passions and leverage social media to your advantage. In short: It will equip you to succeed in our increasingly connected world. With this book as your guide, you will craft a positive personal brand, build a digital dossier, and master real-world skills like networking and interviewing. You will learn how to share your unique talents and perspective with the world — regardless of your path in life.

The core of *Brand Up* focuses on the high school years, where personal branding and digital savvy first become imperative. It has never been more essential for teens to use digital media and develop a personal brand online. A positive digital footprint can open doors to desired colleges and coveted first jobs — but a negative digital footprint can cause irreparable harm.

It's often said that life is a journey, not a destination. While this can be true, teens need to think about their destination at this seminal juncture in their lives. Where do you see yourself in ten years? What kind of person do you want to be? What kind of career do you want to have — an engineer, a fitness instructor, an entrepreneur, or perhaps an astronaut? Maybe you want to work for a major corporation, or maybe you want to start your own business.

Along the way to your destination, expect obstacles — from pandemics to social injustice. It's not easy growing up in these times, which is all the more reason to stay true to yourself and pursue your passions and goals with zest. Keep your eye on the destination and stay on course. No matter what your destination is, *Brand Up* will give you the roadmap you need to get there. So buckle up and enjoy the ride!

All the best,

Stacey Ross Cohen

INTRODUCTION

Let's start by revisiting your childhood. You probably first learned the power of being "Uniquely You" from a familiar branding expert: Dr. Seuss. That's right: The bestselling author of *The Cat and the Hat* was ahead of his time, popularizing quips like "Today you are you, that is truer than true. There is no one alive who is youer than you." Dr. Seuss is a fun read; he's also a reminder to always stand out and be unique. That's the essence of *Brand Up*, too.

Who Should Read This?

This book is for all teens, not just high-achieving, type-A kids who want to go to an Ivy League college and work at a Fortune 100 company. There are many paths to success that don't involve attending an elite university. It is also for those who wish to enter a trade (e.g., hairdressing, carpentry) or who want to become the next TikTok star. Those feeling lost, overwhelmed, or just plain confused about the future can equally benefit. This book will help you — whoever you are — create a roadmap to success.

Why Read This?

It has never been more essential to build a personal brand early. It's how you put your best self out there to score scholarships, snag internships, land jobs, and more. Personal branding is more than just an online profile — it's a holistic picture that can make or break everything from college admissions to career opportunities.

Brand Up will put you well ahead of the curve when it comes to personal branding. You will better understand yourself, develop a growth mindset, and learn how to succeed in any situation. You will become a master of first impressions and stand out from the crowd.

How? The book features bite-size expertise, anecdotes, and wisdom from educators, entrepreneurs, and students who successfully built stellar brands themselves. Author Stacey Ross Cohen also scoured the globe to get invaluable insights from more than 40 college admission officers and educational consultants on what colleges are looking for in applicants and how to get an edge in college admissions. (Did you know that a college admissions officer spends an average of *just ten minutes* on each application?)

There are also chapters dedicated to LinkedIn, networking, doing good, and entrepreneurship — all critical real-world skills. I provide exercises, tips, and insights on everything from creating a positive social media presence to goal-setting to interview skills. And I include essential templates, like sample thank you letters to send to college admissions officers and job recruiters.

Read on so we can start building your future now.

How Do I Use This Book?

This 190-page playbook is packed with information, including exercises, mini-quizzes, writing activities, and a resource section for your college and career journey. Don't be overwhelmed: Whether used in a classroom setting or individually, the playbook is not designed to be completed in one sitting. The book is divided into sections. Since the exercises are designed to be completed in order, you'll get the most out of them if you finish them in sequence. Finally, the book is most effective when you can focus your full attention on it, so it's best to complete it when you won't be interrupted.

The best way to find success is to forge your own path, so I encourage you to take what you need from this book and make it your own. And if you find that some of the advice doesn't work for you, don't be afraid to modify it or even ignore it entirely. Now go out there and make your own story — and make it count.

What If I Can't Do It?

We've all been there before. We're faced with a new challenge, and we can't help but wonder: What if I fail? It's natural to second-guess ourselves, especially when stepping out of our comfort zone. You're not going to break if you don't follow every step perfectly. Instead, think of the book as a source of inspiration. Use it to open your eyes to new possibilities and remind yourself that you're capable of so much more than you realize.

Won't This Make Me Look Just Like Everyone Else?

No! In fact, this book is about just the opposite — taking control of your brand and standing out from the competition. Far from making you look like everyone else, this playbook will help you put your best, most authentic foot forward to shine uniquely. Take it from someone who is a twin: the best compliment I have ever received is *you are unique!* As a twin, my struggle to cultivate my own identity made me more sensitive to the need to develop one's uniqueness. And if I can do it, so can you!

Making a Name for Yourself

Brand Up: The Ultimate Playbook for College & Career Success in the Digital World empowers teens to build a positive personal brand and digital dossier, regardless of their desired path in life. The playbook provides teens with strategies, tools, and exercises to uncover their strengths and passions and leverage social media to their advantage. Why? Because personal branding is now essential. It's more than just an online profile — it's a holistic picture that can make or break college admissions, career opportunities, scholarships, and more.

Although it may appear that personal brands "just happen," they don't. An intentional effort is needed to identify, refine, and broadcast your skills and interests. Those who actively tend to their online presence early and often exponentially increase their likelihood of success later, from college admissions to that all-important first job. The ideal time to begin personal branding is in high school, as you interact with people who can impact your life in outsized ways, such as college admissions counselors, athletic coaches, employers, recruiters, and others.

Personal branding and digital savvy are more critical than ever. It's never been so essential to shape your online presence and make a mark in our hyper-connected world. Here's why:

College admissions are no longer based solely on test scores, transcripts, and essays. In fact, a growing number of colleges are joining the test-optional movement and ending requirements that applicants even submit SAT and ACT scores. It's become clear what teens post online influences the college admissions process. According to Kaplan's 2021 survey, 66 percent of college admissions officers think that applicants' social media posts are "fair game" to help them determine who gets in.

Online presence affects employment. A strong online presence is equally important for those seeking employment or planning to take a gap year before heading to college. Employers scope out candidates' social media and online presence to determine good "fit" qualities during the hiring process. Most human resource professionals claim that they have withheld job offers when inappropriate social media content is discovered. Similarly, the majority of employers and recruiters use social media to find talent. LinkedIn is a prime source for recruiting entry-level students.

Youth entrepreneurship is on the rise. Business success can be achieved at any age. The pandemic, coupled with the soaring gig economy and technology shifts, has made it easier (and desirable) for teens to start their own businesses.

Digital savvy is a critical skill requiring you to put your best foot forward online. Even a superficial scan by an admissions counselor or prospective employer may reveal ugly things: racist or sexist comments, bullying, beer-chugging photos, and so on. When you *don't* use good judgment, the consequences can be severe. Consider Harvard's withdrawal of admission offers to ten incoming freshmen for offensive Facebook posts in 2017. This reminds us that "smart" kids are not always smart on social media. Similar social media hazards seem to play out regularly in the news. Suffice it to say that social media sleuthing is here to stay. Assume others will mine social media accounts to find bombshells, especially college coaches and employers recruiting only the best talent.

This book draws on my 25-plus years of experience shaping the brands of high school students, college graduates, CEOs, business owners, entrepreneurs, and others. I'm a storyteller at heart who excels at crafting compelling narratives and possesses the skill to take brands to market. I cherish my gift of leveraging each client's unique voice to make an outsized impact on social media, in board rooms, and everywhere in between. As a twin, cultivating a unique identity wasn't a choice; it was a necessity. The desire to be unique is a sentiment fully familiar to me. My experience as a twin sharpened my ability to stand out in the face of constant comparisons, insensitive remarks, and name mix-ups. The best compliment I ever received growing up was, "Stacey, you are so unique!"

I'm incredibly fortunate to collaborate on this playbook with close business colleagues and contributing authors Jason Shaffer and Alan Katzman, giants in digital leadership and college admissions. I also tap into the wisdom of the experts: web-savvy educators, college admissions officers, entrepreneurs, psychologists, high school guidance counselors, recruiters, and, of course, students who successfully built stellar brands. Throughout the playbook, you'll find concrete, practical pointers complemented by a list of "Brandamentals," or key takeaways, at the end of each section.

I like to refer to this process as **Personal Branding in 3D** because personal branding success boils down to three steps: discovery, development, and delivery. It is also a fitting name since the process creates depth and meaning in our lives.

1. Discovery: During this phase, you will do a lot of self-reflection to determine your "who" and "why." I introduce my Me Squared™ process, which helps map your strengths, passions, goals, and values. I also share popular and helpful personality tests, which can further crystallize what makes you **YOU**. The purpose of all this is to develop a clear, compelling Uniquely Me statement. This is the personal branding message you'll send out into the world.

2. Development: This step involves cleaning up and packaging your online assets to create a shiny digital portfolio. Interview tips and sample thank you letters are part of this step. Emphasis is placed on the most influential personal branding platform of our era: LinkedIn, where some 40 million students and recent graduates mingle with admissions officers, hiring managers, professors, and one another.

3. Delivery: This step shows you how to manage your social media presence and broadcast your personal brand to the world through multiple channels. This section also includes networking essentials to help you establish and grow a strong network to enhance your career prospects. Networking is one of the most powerful tools you can use to achieve academic and professional success.

The goal of *Brand Up* is not only to understand how to use personal branding and social media to your benefit but also how you can do so responsibly while avoiding pitfalls along the way. You'll learn how to build an online brand that reflects who you are, as well as learn what colleges are looking for in applicants today. With this guide in hand, you'll be able to take control of your own brand so that when it comes time for college applications, job hunting, or starting a business, **you will stand out.** So let's start building our future now by learning how to create a positive and professional image online and off.

Personal Branding Quiz: How Fit Is Your Personal Brand and Online Presence?

Let's get started. How does your personal brand measure up?
Try answering these 15 questions:

☐ Have you identified your "it" factor, or what makes you stand out?

☐ What would make an employer or college admission officer choose you out of a large pool of applicants?

☐ Do you know what makes you a good investment?

☐ Do you have a 30-second elevator pitch about yourself?

☐ Do you have a strong online profile/bio?

☐ Do you know how others perceive you?

☐ Who is your target audience (i.e., the people you most want to impress)?

☐ Do you have a personal and/or business brand domain name?

☐ Do you have Google Alert keywords set up to monitor your reputation?

☐ Do you have your privacy settings properly set up in all social networks?

☐ Are you using your name consistently on all social networks?

☐ Do you have a content strategy for your blog and social networks?

☐ Do you have a maintenance plan to review social networks?

☐ Does your personal brand accurately represent who you are?

☐ Do people (other than family and your closest friends) respond favorably to your postings, blogs, and/or webpage?

If you responded "no" or even "not sure" to more than three of these, this book is for you.

Why Personal Branding?

Many people confuse personal brand and personal branding. It's important to understand and distinguish these two terms:

A **personal brand** is the public's perception of you based on the values, strengths, passions, experience, skills, and achievements that you present to the world. A personal brand is more than an online profile or résumé; it is the essence of YOU — the authentic and curated parts of your story that highlight your best self in order to help achieve your goals. A personal brand is created through the strategic process of personal branding.

Personal branding is an intentional effort to identify, shape, and communicate your value. It entails differentiating yourself from the competition to achieve college placement, career success, personal success, thought leadership, or even celebrity status. Personal branding involves honing your narrative to establish an identity, which is then amplified through social media and other channels.

Authentically You

BE REAL.

BE YOU.

BE HUMAN.

BE RELATABLE.

BE VULNERABLE.

The essence of personal branding is about expressing your authentic self and celebrating your individuality. It's about digging deep within yourself to identify the blend of strengths and attributes that make you unique. Personal branding is not about changing who you are or compromising your values. It's about being true to yourself rather than playing a role or creating a character.

Colleges want to get to know the "real you." It's important to showcase your best, most authentic self on your college application, including your strengths, challenges, and dreams.

WORD OF CAUTION:
Avoid tailoring your brand too much to the audience. Make your brand about you first.

Personal Branding Benefits

Personal branding is the marketing of you. You are, in essence, the brand manager and need to play an active role in making the most of what you have to offer. Personal branding is a worthy time investment that comes with the following benefits:

Self-awareness. Uncovering your strengths, talents, passions, and values is a fundamental component of personal growth. Knowing who you are and what value you offer is empowering and gives your life direction and meaning.

Clarity. Once you crystallize who you are and what you want to achieve, you can create a clear roadmap to your destination. Clarity makes it easier to identify goals and take action.

Uniqueness. By recognizing and developing your unique talents, you can distinguish yourself from the competition. In a cluttered market, differentiating yourself is your best chance to succeed.

Confidence. Self-esteem soars from knowing your strengths and the unique value you bring to the world. Having this confidence puts you at ease in social and professional situations. Introducing yourself and sharing your story becomes second nature.

Credibility. Building a solid track record of success begins with living your brand, delivering on your brand promise, and taking actions aligned with the brand. In addition, having others speak on your behalf (e.g., teacher recommendations, job references, testimonials) will reinforce your credibility.

Reputation. A strong, positive personal brand makes you stand out and forms a lasting impression. Consistently sharing your brand through online and offline channels builds recognition and prestige.

Professional advancement. Personal branding yields increased career opportunities, including a higher salary, promotions, rewarding partnerships, new clients, and business opportunities.

Portability. Personal brands are portable. You can take your brand with you wherever life takes you.

It's your choice: Do you want to control the narrative or let your online reputation take on a life of its own? Embrace personal branding.

The Origins of Personal Branding

The phrase "personal branding" was coined in the late '90s by management guru Tom Peters. In 1997, Peters wrote in a *Fast Company* article:

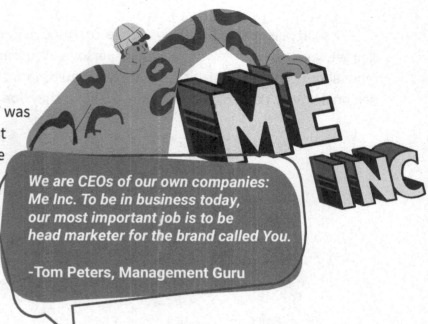

We are CEOs of our own companies: Me Inc. To be in business today, our most important job is to be head marketer for the brand called You.

-Tom Peters, Management Guru

You Have a Brand: It's Time to Own It

Everybody has a personal brand, and it's either positive, negative, or neutral. Personal brands are complex and shaped by our skills, achievements, interests, and creative output. But at the foundation of any personal brand is a singular trait: our reputation. Without a positive reputation, no personal brand can flourish. If you're not viewed as a dependable and trustworthy individual, your talents and experience — no matter how impressive — won't matter much. And in today's digital world, where images, social media profiles, and news stories are immortal, upholding a sterling reputation is more important than ever. One hiccup, whether an awkward photo, an unforgiving article, or an inappropriate post, can haunt someone for years.

While some opt to ignore their personal brand and let it develop with little or no regard, those ahead of the game understand that they need to nurture and monitor their personal brand and present their best selves consistently across multiple online and offline channels.

The principles of personal branding are very similar to building a business brand. First, you need to get inside the target market's mindset and answer the question: "What's in it for me?" Effective brand marketing talks about benefits — the value that a product or service brings to the end user (the customer) — rather than features. Let's take Greek yogurt as an example. You could highlight features, like the yogurt brand celebrating its 25th anniversary or its ten grams of protein. But it's far more advantageous to emphasize the yogurt's ***benefits:*** consumers will be healthier, live longer, and reduce digestive issues. Which one would you buy? It's no surprise that most consumers — whether choosing yogurt, a new hair salon, or sneakers — are drawn to the benefits.

A solid personal brand allows you to cut through that clutter and stand out. Maybe it's your skill set, your point of view, an engaging personality, or simply your creativity. Personal branding is not about blending in or sticking with the status quo. Instead, weave your uniqueness into your personal brand. Think Beyoncé, Oprah, or Drake: they don't even need a second name!

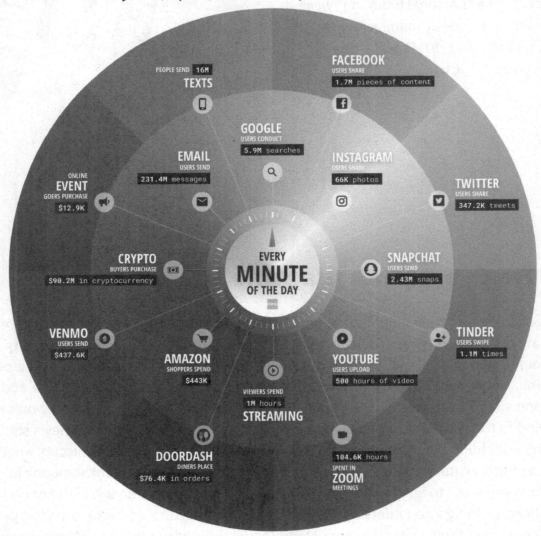

Data Never Sleeps Report, Domo, 2022 – Reprinted with Permission

Consider this: there are approximately 5.9 million Google searches per minute (Data Never Sleeps Report, Domo, 2022). When someone searches you, you want to greet them with positive, appealing, honest, and consistent accounts of yourself. It's not about bragging — it's about what you have to offer and how you want to present that to the world.

This doesn't mean you need the polished look of an advertising agency, nor does it mean you must present your brand in a formal or stuffy manner. A little fun, even humor, and certainly a sparkling personality can attract positive attention. But you always need to run your brand through the PURE Test: Is it **P**ositive, **U**nbiased, **R**espectful, and **E**thical? Another filter is the Grandma Test: What would your grandmother say? Would she find it funny/entertaining or offensive and inappropriate? The point is this: if you're not 100 percent sure about posting something after running it through these two tests, then run it past someone who is not in your immediate circle of peers for a second opinion.

Still, even in a digital era, personal branding is much more than just an "online thing." It's about the mark you make in the physical world, too:

- Your aspirations, ideals, insights, and achievements.
- The contributions you make to your team and community.
- The causes you champion.
- The hearts you warm and the smiles you bring to faces around you.

No matter what stage of life you're in or your goals, personal branding is no longer a luxury, something that only Hollywood publicists do for the stars. Indeed, students and job applicants are expected to have several personal brand assets, including a résumé, a LinkedIn profile, and a portfolio of their work.

In fact, it's a personal brand that often gets a business off the ground. Frequently young entrepreneurs seek investors or venture capitalists. But what is it that those investors or venture capitalists look for? A new product or a new service? Not necessarily. They look at the person *behind* the product or service. They want to put their money behind someone they can trust to make that business a success. That takes us right back to the personal brand. Investors will research that aspiring entrepreneur carefully, and it's less likely they will shell out hundreds of thousands of dollars, or even millions of dollars, to someone with a sketchy or questionable personal brand. And don't fool yourself: If you're starting your own business at age 21, that inappropriate comment or photo you posted online at 15 can still come back to hurt you.

There's no doubt that personal branding is here to stay. It is becoming more embedded in the fabric of everything from academics to entrepreneurship to the workplace.

Personal Branding Myth-Busting:

Time for a true-false exercise. Let's bust some myths about personal branding

False: Those who practice personal branding are narcissists and braggarts

True: Personal branding is not about *me, me, me* It's mainly about the value you bring to others

False: Personal branding is just for celebrities and those who want to become famous

True: Personal branding is for everyone: the college-bound, the career seekers, the CEOs, and everyone in between

False: Personal branding is all about having a big presence on social media with many followers

True: While social media can amplify your brand, a solid social media presence alone does not equal a strong personal brand

False: Personal brands are short-lived

True: Personal branding is a lifelong effort — one that's constantly evolving and requires regular maintenance

False: Personal branding is a fad

True: Personal branding is here to stay — the internet has cemented its importance

Putting Your Best Digital Foot Forward

Today, the digital footprint one leaves on the internet is the encapsulation of their personal brand. A positive digital footprint can open doors to top colleges and coveted first jobs. But a negative digital footprint can cause lasting harm. We all have a digital footprint, a bundle of information (photos, blog posts, social media handles, online profiles, etc.) that shows up when we Google ourselves — or, more likely, when someone else Googles us. But the term "digital footprint" is a bit misleading. Footprints fade away. Digital footprints, however, can last forever. They are visible to anyone, anywhere. Online photos, social media profiles, and news stories are permanent and discoverable, which means managing your online reputation is no longer optional. You must take control of your narrative, or someone else most certainly will.

Most of us couldn't have predicted that so much of our lives would be visible one day. It's important to remember that social networks may *seem* private but are indeed public. There are consequences for what you post, even if your intentions aren't malicious. Many teens assume they can conceal their Instagram accounts behind aliases, with little awareness of how deeply professionals can dig. As it turns out, that quick snap doing bong hits on spring break in Florida may come back to haunt you.

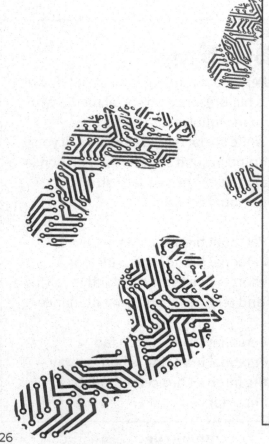

BRANDAMENTALS

Commit these top takeaways to memory:

1 While the term "personal branding" may be relatively new, the concept is age-old. The importance of a sterling reputation to academic and professional success is nothing new.

2 The internet makes personal branding imperative. At a time when every photo and comment can live forever in pixels, it's critical to tend to your brand carefully.

3 Personal branding isn't about boasting. That's a common misconception. Rather, it's about showing others how you can help them achieve their goals.

4 Personal branding should start early to build momentum for college admissions and job interviews.

SECTION A:
DISCOVERY

PART I – WHO ARE YOU ANYWAY?

Self-Awareness Is All That

Let's talk about an essential trait that pertains to all aspects of personal branding: self-awareness. Research shows that self-awareness is a leading predictor of success in one's life. Those with a high level of self-awareness — who have a strong grasp of their passions, strengths, weaknesses, and values — are at an advantage and achieve greater academic and career success. In fact, self-awareness has been cited as the most important capability for leaders to develop, according to the authors of "How to Become a Better Leader" *(MIT Sloan Management Review, 2012)*, who conducted more than 2000 in-depth conversations with international executives.

It won't come as a surprise, then, that self-awareness is the foundation of personal branding. I spoke with one of the leading experts on exactly this: Dr. Tasha Eurich, organizational psychologist, author of *Insight: The Surprising Truth About How Others See Us, How We See Ourselves, and Why the Answers Matter More Than We Think*, and the creator of a TED Talk on this same topic. In our conversation, Dr. Eurich explained that self-awareness has two components: *Internal self-awareness* is about understanding yourself — your passions, values, aspirations, strengths, and weaknesses. *External self-awareness* is about understanding how others perceive you.

Reality check: Dr. Eurich revealed that most of us are not as self-aware as we think. Her research team found that 95 percent of people consider themselves self-aware, but the real number is closer to 10 percent or 15 percent. One reason for the "shortfall" is our lack of external self-awareness. As Dr. Eurich points out, "External awareness is a critical skill and more difficult to achieve than an internal perspective. We need to take the time to understand the point-of-view of others, which can give us a much more objective view of ourselves."

How else can we discover the hidden strengths that give us a unique edge? Of course, other people will perceive you in a variety of ways, depending on how well they know you and in what circumstances you interact with them. For example, your football or cheerleading coach, your student advisor, and your boss at an after-school job may see different aspects of your personality. By understanding how different people view your actions, your behaviors, and how you present yourself, you can incorporate the best traits that others see in you while avoiding negative characteristics and behaviors. This kind of self-awareness will increase your chance of being perceived in the best manner.

Those whose self-image aligns with the image they want to present can reap enormous benefits. "There is strong scientific evidence that people who know themselves and how others see them are happier. Self-aware people are better performers at work, more confident communicators, and achieve greater success academically and career-wise," says Dr. Eurich. It's clear that the famed Greek philosopher Socrates was onto something when he said, "To know thyself is the beginning of wisdom."

Although many of us aren't as self-aware as we think, there's good news: Dr. Eurich believes self-awareness is an "infinitely learnable skill" and says that we're never too young to start. Indeed, high school is an ideal time to take a deep dive. Dr. Eurich encourages high school students to explore personality tests to assess and improve self-awareness.

So how do you increase self-awareness? Regular, objective reflection is key. And there is broad agreement among experts that journaling and mindfulness are best practices for this. We will cover mindfulness and positive affirmations in the next section. And now we are ready to embark on the Discovery phase of **Building Your Personal Brand in 3D: Discovery, Development, Delivery.**

Strong brands begin by defining themselves. The exercises that follow will help you determine what you do well, what you love to do, your identity, and your vision. This all starts with a self-audit to pinpoint your purpose, strengths, values, and passion. It's essential to crystallize your uniqueness — or competitive advantage — and why you're a worthy investment. Average just doesn't cut it.

The first essential task is to find your "wow" factor, the unique aspect of your character, intellect, or achievements that will make your target audience sit up and take notice. Let's get started on uncovering your "wow" factor. **Remember: Personal branding is not a matter of *me-me-me* — it's about your value to others.**

The path to establishing your personal brand should begin with deep reflection. Ask yourself: Who am I? How did I get here? What do I have to give? Whatever it is I want to do, what will it take to succeed in this life?

In this section, I introduce some warm-up exercises followed by my tried-and-true method Me Squared™ — a self-audit — to develop your brand from the ground up. This fun and engaging exercise culminates in a "Uniquely Me" statement: The distinct personal branding message that you can send out into the world. (In traditional marketing, we call this a "UVP," or unique value proposition.) Also included is a list of personality tests that can further hone what makes you you. Now, let's get started.

Personal branding allows you to figure out why someone should choose YOU!

Why do YOU stand out from the host of other college applicants?

Why should YOU be selected for that internship at Google?

Why should YOU get hired for a part-time job?

Why should someone invest in YOUR business idea?

A fundamental step in developing one's brand is to figure out who you really are (your soft and hard skills, achievements, values, passions), who you want to reach (your target audience), and how you differ from the competition.

Warm-up Exercises

Creating a personal brand requires us to become storytellers. Social media posts, video uploads, blogs, and even our offline encounters are a collection of the stories we have experienced and chosen to share. When reflecting on the power of one's story, consider Mister Rogers' Neighborhood television host Fred Rogers, who once admitted to carrying a note in his pocket each day with a quote he heard from a social worker. That note read, "**Frankly, there isn't anyone you cannot learn to love, once you know their story.**"

This is what building a brand is all about. Use your stories and their uniqueness to connect with others. Motivate them. Inspire them. Help them to fall in love with themselves and, ultimately, with you. When presenting this to students, their response is often, "Okay, so what stories should I tell?" or "I'm just a kid, I have never done anything special, so what can I possibly offer?" Although this answer will not be the same for everyone, the inspiration for these stories derives from the same place — **your past.**

Activity: The Identity Mirror

As we kick off the first series of activities, you will be asked to reflect on HOW you became the person you are today.

We must begin with a look in the mirror. Self-reflection starts by looking inward and asking questions about who we are and what's important to us — questions like, "How can I best live my day-to-day life in order to achieve these goals that matter most?" The importance of self-reflection cannot be overstated. It is necessary for personal growth and development and has many benefits that extend beyond our own lives into the world at large — for example, by making us more insightful leaders who can affect change in others' lives.

We will also consider the people, places, and moments that have inspired and influenced you. The person, or persons, may be a teacher, mentor, friend, family member, or if you are lucky enough, all of the above. Ask yourself: How has this person made a meaningful impact in my life? What did I learn from them? Was the relationship a reciprocal one?

Perhaps you have been lucky enough to travel the globe. If not, perhaps your greatest memories occurred in your neighborhood, school, or on your favorite sports field. Regardless of the place, the memories that you've created have helped frame your thinking and motivations.

We can use these memories of lessons learned and hurdles overcome in our storytelling.

Finally, consider those specific moments in life that have led you to where you are now. The birth of a sibling, a relative's death, a difficult breakup, and a glowing award all leave a mark. These defining moments will provide others a glimpse into your most sacred memories and help you connect with others who may relate. As you begin this process, remember that this is not a race, there are no wrong answers, and what you share is private only to you. Good luck and have fun rediscovering your past.

Use the space below to share the names of people who you most admire and who have had the most influence on your life.

_____   _____

_____   _____

_____   _____

_____   _____

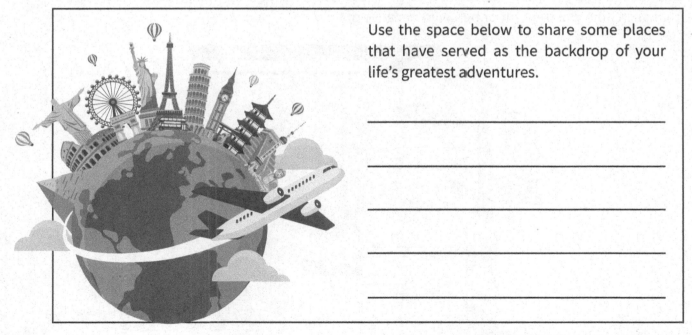

Use the space below to share some places that have served as the backdrop of your life's greatest adventures.

_____

_____

_____

_____

_____

Share key moments (good and/or bad) that have shaped
who you are today.

_____

_____

_____

_____

Now that you have taken the time to generate some ideas about the people, places, and moments that have brought you to where you are today, let us see how we can use these to craft a meaningful story and serve as an inspiration to others.

On the following pages, several prompts will be provided to help you go into further detail about some of the people, places, and moments that you have shared. Write what YOU want! A story, poem, drawing, or anything else that helps you think more deeply about the prompts and, more importantly, the inspiration behind each of your answers.

However you choose to express yourself and your stories, remember that this process requires us to consider every detail and decision. Try to get at the root of why you have chosen this specific story in your answers. What was the lesson? What is so memorable? Was there a change in how you thought or behaved because of this?

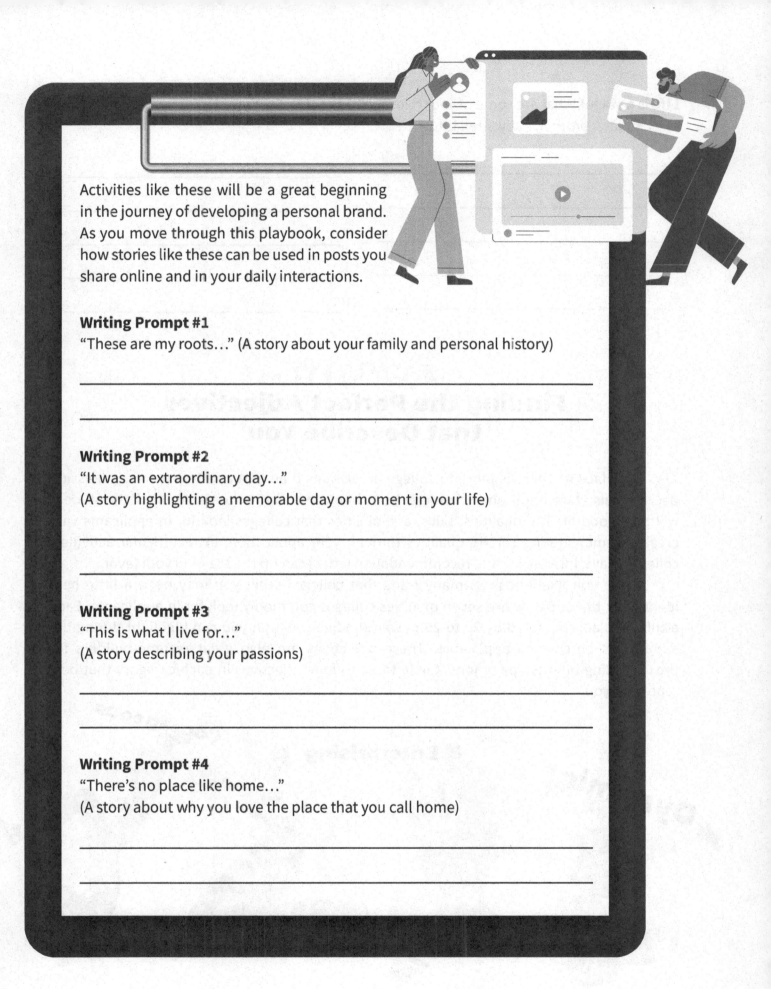

Activities like these will be a great beginning in the journey of developing a personal brand. As you move through this playbook, consider how stories like these can be used in posts you share online and in your daily interactions.

Writing Prompt #1
"These are my roots…" (A story about your family and personal history)

_____

_____

Writing Prompt #2
"It was an extraordinary day…"
(A story highlighting a memorable day or moment in your life)

_____

_____

Writing Prompt #3
"This is what I live for…"
(A story describing your passions)

_____

_____

Writing Prompt #4
"There's no place like home…"
(A story about why you love the place that you call home)

_____

_____

Life is a stage! What are some of your roles? List **ten roles** you play in life (e.g., athlete, brother, babysitter, tutor).

1. _____
2. _____
3. _____
4. _____
5. _____

6. _____
7. _____
8. _____
9. _____
10. _____

ACTIVITY:
Finding the Perfect Adjectives that Describe You

Let's face it. There is more to college admissions than GPA and test scores. Admission decisions also take applicants' character traits into consideration to determine if the student will be a good fit. The qualities, skills, and abilities that colleges look for in applicants vary greatly. Demonstrating certain qualities through your application, extracurricular activities, college essays, interviews, and recommendation letters can tip the scales in your favor.

While you likely possess many traits that colleges seek, you may need a little help identifying them. Below are seven qualities colleges commonly look for in applicants. Each attribute is accompanied by 20 to 25 powerful adjectives that you can highlight during the admissions process as applicable. These adjectives are also great résumé-builders for those seeking internships or jobs. Circle three to four adjectives in each category that best represent you.

Leadership. A leader is on the front lines and helps others achieve goals. In high school, leadership shows itself in many ways: student government, athletics, tutoring, volunteer activities, clubs, and more. College applicants with strong leadership skills are viewed favorably. You can use leadership adjectives as a way to demonstrate your ability to oversee projects, manage teams, and guide others to success.

Leadership Adjectives

Assertive	Determined	Enterprising	Dynamic	Courageous
Influential	Bold	Solution-oriented	Problem-solver	Accomplished
Reliable	Competent	Responsible	Goal-oriented	Impactful
Resilient	Passionate	Inspiring	Confident	Accountable
Proactive	Decisive	Enthusiastic	Persistent	

Creativity. The ability to think outside the box can be applied to any field, from the arts to business to technology. Many colleges value innovative and creative thinkers and consider it an important trait. Employers likewise seek candidates who can think of novel solutions to problems.

Creativity Adjectives

Cutting-edge	Leading-edge	Inventive	Forward-looking	Innovative
Inspired	Imaginative	Creative	Artistic	Unique
Forward-thinking	Ground-breaking	Ingenious	Exclusive	Revolutionary
Advanced	Breakthrough	Progressive	Original	Visionary

Team Player. A team player contributes to their group to meet shared goals. While individual accomplishments are important, colleges also place a high value on collaboration in group settings (e.g., performing arts, volunteer work, and clubs). Strong collaborative skills are essential for academic and professional success. The adjectives below will help you showcase your teamwork credentials to admissions officers.

Team Player Adjectives

Amiable	Amicable	Tolerant	Collective	Combined
United	Joint	Associated	Shared	Integrated
Respectful	Diplomatic	Cooperative	Supportive	Harmonious
Cheerful	Congenial	Receptive	Welcoming	Courteous
Collaborative	Communicative	Connected	Team-minded	

Work Ethic. Hard work and perseverance are key ingredients to success. Perhaps it was said best by the late Colin Powell, former Secretary of State: "A dream does not become a reality through magic; it takes sweat, determination, and hard work." Colleges seek students who demonstrate drive and commitment to their academic, extracurricular, and personal goals.

Work Ethic Adjectives

Diligent	Grit	Tenacious	Self-starter	Ambitious
Determined	Self-motivated	Organized	Methodical	Detail-oriented
Enthusiastic	Dedicated	Passionate	Enterprising	Driven
Persistent	Energetic	Systematic	Committed	Motivated
Prepared	Disciplined	Focused		

Critical Thinking. Colleges seek to create a student body of curious, inquisitive minds with a passion for learning and the ability to analyze information. Critical thinking is a highly desirable trait among applicants, particularly in pursuing degrees like engineering, political science, or business. Make sure to shine a light on activities (e.g., debate team, research projects) that highlight critical or analytical thinking.

Critical Thinking Adjectives

Inquiring	Precise	Methodical	Investigative	Curious
Questioning	Inquisitive	Analytical	Problem-solving	Progressive
Challenging	Persistent	Diligent	Meticulous	Inventive
Intellectual	Logical	Discerning	Detail-oriented	Knowledgeable
Perceptive	Thorough	Insightful		

Open-Minded. College exposes you to new opportunities to engage with a wide variety of ideas, people, subjects, and viewpoints that differ from your own. Colleges value the ability to venture out of your comfort zone and take risks to advance your knowledge and skills base. Workplaces also value those who are nimble and adaptable.

Open-Minded Adjectives

Agile	Capable	Perceptive	Nimble	Versatile
Resourceful	Dynamic	Responsive	Flexible	Positive
Broad-minded	Adaptable	Tolerant	Accepting	Multifaceted
Quick-thinking	Flexible	Unbiased	Receptive	Comprehensive
Energetic	Prompt	Diverse		

Socially Conscious. Colleges and employers seek applicants who care about the world and want to make an impact. There are many ways to demonstrate concern for others through service, including supporting local food banks, environmental clean-up, and tutoring struggling students. Engaging in community service allows students to acquire essential life skills and has a lasting, positive impact on the community.

Socially Conscious Adjectives

Empathetic	Generous	Contributing	Caring	Philanthropic
Charitable	Considerate	Responsive	Perceptive	Compassionate
Altruistic	Supportive	Humanitarian	Understanding	Engaging
Sympathetic	Sensitive	Feeling	Accommodating	Cooperative

Many schools list desired traits on their websites, so research what each school values in their student body. While no magic words will put your application at the top of the stack, distinct and engaging adjectives will certainly help it stand out. The bottom line is to make every word count and demonstrate your traits with tangible examples in your application and interactions with each college.

Me Squared™: Self-Audit

So, now that you are warmed up, let's get ready to answer the question: "Why choose me?" We will take our learnings from the Identity Mirror and employ the Me Squared process, my proprietary method for mapping core values and generating a "Uniquely Me" statement.

Exercise:

Here is the Me Squared quadrant and accompanying directions for each quadrant:

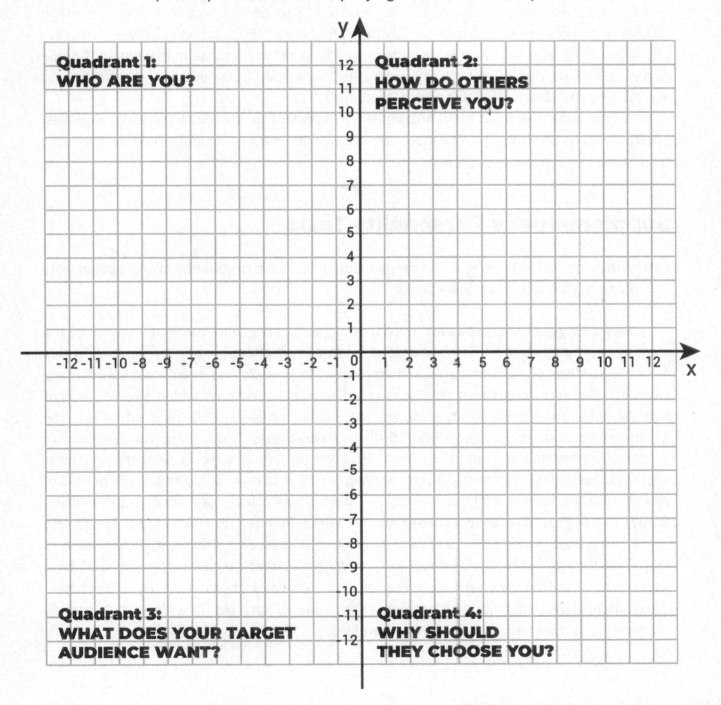

Quadrant 1: WHO ARE YOU?

Review the previous section, "Understanding Your Perfect Adjectives." Generate ten adjectives or phrases that describe your core strengths, then place them in Quadrant 1. These can be soft skills (e.g., adaptable, enthusiastic) and hard skills (e.g., artificial intelligence, video production). Both soft and hard skills are essential to your college and career readiness. High school students do not typically have many hard skills, so no worries if you fall short in this area. Finally, make sure you put an asterisk by your superpower — that is, your number one trait.

Here's an example of this exercise: Meet Peter, a 17-year-old high school junior who aspires to be an engineer. His dad is an architect, and he has met and talked to many engineers growing up. Peter listed five adjectives for his soft skills: analytical, driven, creative, positive, and enterprising. And he recorded three hard skills: database management, Google Analytics, and UX design. Peter's superpower is "analytical," as he excels and is passionate about problem-solving. He places this in Quadrant 1.

A final note about this quadrant: While it's important to understand one's weaknesses, I prefer to focus on strengths. The more you can play to your talents and strengths, the more readily you can perform at your peak.

Supplementary Personality Tests

OPTIONAL: You may want to consider supplementing the exercise above by taking a personality test. Here are a few of the top-ranked tests:

Myers-Briggs Type Indicator (MBTI) (myersbriggs.org and mbtionline.com) is the most popular personality test worldwide. It's used in 26 countries and by more than two million individuals — from students and employees to soldiers and even potential marriage partners. The test consists of 90-plus "forced choice" questions, which provide insight into the subject's perception, decision-making, leadership skills, and other attributes. The questionnaire segments subjects into 16 distinct personality types, using combinations of the following designations: Introvert (I) vs. Extrovert (E); Intuitive (N) vs. Sensory (S); Thinking (T) vs. Feeling (F); Perceiving (P) vs. Judging (J). For example, if you're an "ENFP" (Extroverted, Intuitive, Feeling, and Perceiving) type, here is how you are described on the website: "Enthusiastic innovators, always seeing new possibilities in the world around them. Their world is full of possible projects or interests they want to pursue. Imaginative, high-spirited, and ingenious, they are often able to do almost anything that interests them. They are confident, spontaneous, and flexible, and often rely on their ability to improvise. They value home, family, friendships, creativity, and learning." The results of each test provide a list of specific occupations that are compatible with one's profile.

CliftonStrengthsAssessment (formerly called the ClifttonStrengthsFinder) gallup.com/cliftonstrengths is a popular web-based personality assessment that measures natural aptitudes in interpersonal skills, leadership abilities, and creative potential in 34 different areas. It is based on the research of psychologist Don Clifton and was developed by Gallup, Inc. The Clifton Strengths assessment takes approximately 30 minutes to complete and presents 177 items/questions (20 seconds to respond to each item). Each item consists of a pair of potential self-descriptors, such as "I read instructions carefully" versus "I like to jump right into things." The in-depth report highlights your top five strengths, which can help you advance your goals, address challenges, and develop your strengths.

Enneagram (enneagraminstitute.com) is based on an ancient body of wisdom that identifies nine core personality types (The Reformer; The Helper; The Achiever; The Individualist; The Investigator; The Loyalist; The Enthusiast; The Challenger; and The Peacemaker) and how each sees and interacts with the world. The Enneagram system believes that each of us has a dominant personality type inside of us that drives how we think, behave, learn, see the world, and evolve. The test is about recognizing our core drivers and the impact of our experiences, motivations, attitudes, and fears.

16 Personalities: (16personalities.com) is one of the most popular personality quizzes online, with over 26 million tests taken. And it takes fewer than 12 minutes to complete. Based on MBTI, the 60-question, free-of-charge personality test assesses who you really are by asking you to indicate how much you agree with statements like "You cannot stand chaos." Like the classic MBTI, your answers determine where you fall on four spectrums: extroverted/introverted, sensing/intuitive, thinking/feeling, and judging/perceiving. At the end, your personality type is provided. Many reviews on the test describe it as fun, engaging, and accurate.

If you opted to take a personality test, be sure to integrate these findings with the ones you have reflected on in the previous section. Are the results in sync?

Quadrant 2: HOW DO OTHERS PERCEIVE YOU?

Face it: We all have personal blind spots. We don't always correctly see how the outside world reads us. The true measure of your brand comes from self-reflection combined with feedback from those who know you best. Just as we conduct a focus group in traditional marketing to understand how consumers view a brand, you need to determine how others view you. It is prudent to seek feedback to continually fill that gap. If you don't, you're limiting your potential, career, and success.

It is equally important to understand what your audience expects or wants from you, as well as what they need, how they function, and what drives them to take action. The impression we give is often made before we even walk in the door. Google can be our best friend or our worst enemy when it comes to personal branding. It has become our new reference check — those vetting you often start there when searching for information about you.

> *Your brand is what people say about you when you're not in the room.*
>
> *–Jeff Bezos, Founder, Amazon*

So, what is the best way to get feedback? Here are three tips from Dr. Eurich to get you started:

1 **Select three to five "loving critics" who will provide honest and supportive feedback.** Teens should pick a family member, close friend, teacher, or coach who understands them well.

2 **Be specific about what you want to know.** Ask your "loving critics" to repeat the same exercise you completed in Quadrant 1 — to list your strengths and soft and hard skills. (Don't forget to ask them to asterisk your superpower.)

3 **Establish a habit of "The Daily Check-In."** Ask yourself daily: What went well today? What didn't go well? And what can I do to be smarter tomorrow? Dr. Eurich believes that by taking time to reflect on your day, you'll better understand yourself and how you relate to others.

Now, armed with information from your "loving critics," fill out Quadrant 2 (see page 41). Does your self-assessment dovetail with the feedback you received? Circle similar adjectives.

Let's return to Peter to once again see this exercise in practice. Peter's "loving critics" are his uncle, a Chemistry teacher, a high school guidance counselor, a neighbor, and a friend. He sent them an email explaining his motivations and posed the following questions:

1) **What are my five strengths?**
2) **What is my superpower (a quality that truly sets me apart) out of these five strengths?**

Peter's five strengths and superpowers are listed to the right. Note that we have a "superpower" match with "analytical."

**Analytical
Driven
Creative
Positive
Enterprising**

Quadrant 3:
WHAT DOES YOUR TARGET AUDIENCE WANT?

One phrase you'll frequently hear during your college search is "best fit"— that is, the school whose academic reputation, areas of study, location, size, and perhaps even Greek life are most appealing to you.

College admissions officers are also looking for the "best fit." Admissions officers spend, on average, just ten minutes per college application — which means you need to make a strong impression fast. The bottom line is that admissions officers want to see what value a student will bring to their campus. As mentioned previously, qualities admissions officers are seeking include leadership skills, determination, curiosity, adaptability, communications savvy, and a devotion to public service.

In this example, we will use college admissions officers as your target audience — which brings us to Quadrant 3. Feel free to switch up your target audience based on your situation.

There are two steps to completing this section:

1 **Identify your target audience**, which might be college admissions officers but also athletic coaches or employers. In short: Who are you trying to impress? For purposes of this exercise, let's stick with college admissions officers. You can expect better results when you identify your target audience and center your messaging on their wants and needs. Feel free to repeat this exercise with a different target audience.

2 **What is your target audience looking for?** As mentioned previously, college admissions officers seek applicants who are a good fit for their community. But let's get more specific. Every school is unique — why not sleuth and see if you can get some intelligence on your dream school? After all, you are so much more than your grades, test scores, and activities. In order to present your best self, you need to get into the college admissions mindset and consider how to present yourself through the written parts of the application (and also in-person or video interviews). Be sure to keep track of your findings.

Okay — time to fill in Quadrant 3 (see page 41). Pick five or so attributes that your desired college(s) value in their applicants.

Let's bring back Peter, who intends on applying to engineering school. His dream school is MIT. The good news is that you can find out what admissions officers seek with a quick search. In fact, there is a landing page: mitadmissions.org/apply/process/what-we-look-for/, which lists key components that drive MIT's selection process: alignment with MIT's mission; collaborative and cooperative spirit; initiative; hands-on creativity; intensity, curiosity, and excitement; character; and the ability to prioritize balance. Peter used the above descriptors and added in "analytical," since it's his "superpower" and relevant to his choice of major, engineering.

Quadrant 4: WHY SHOULD THEY CHOOSE YOU?

In the college selection process, you need to be able to answer this question from admissions officers: "What is it that makes you unique, and how will you contribute to the life of our campus?" Start by gathering intelligence on your competition and what they offer — and then identify your points of difference. Next, consider speaking to a few existing students or recent alumni who can highlight the student body's key characteristics. Why should you be selected over other applicants for that coveted slot? What distinctive benefits do you bring to your audience?

As mentioned before, this process isn't so different from positioning a consumer product. Great companies create value propositions for their products. They define how the product is different in ways that their target audience values. Of course, value propositions go beyond just products — **your personal value proposition is at the heart of your career strategy.**

For Quadrant 4, please review all the previous quadrants and mull over the two to three things that answer the question "Why Choose Me?" Then write them down (see page 41). In his Quadrant 4, Peter listed the following "Why Choose Me?" adjectives: driven, analytical, and leader.

Bravo! You've finished the more difficult part of personal branding. Last but not least, let's develop your Uniquely Me statement.

Uniquely Me Statement

So what is a Uniquely Me statement? It's a memorable, concise blurb describing who you are and what you have to offer. Think of it as your elevator pitch, brand mantra, or tagline, which can be applied to various professional situations. You need to make sure to include this statement in all touchpoints and conversations, including — but not limited to — emails, career fairs, cover letters, LinkedIn profiles, interviews, and essays. These statements typically begin with "I am," "I help," or "I work with."

To start, closely examine your four quadrants, paying particular attention to your unique promise in Quadrant 4. Next, see how you can combine them into one to two short sentences and less than 25 words. Here are a few examples of Uniquely Me statements to get you thinking:

I enjoy applying my creative problem-solving skills to produce beautiful artwork that sparks joy and inspiration.
- Fashion Student

I'm a dedicated team player and goal-getter who motivates others to do their best.
- Athlete

Also, make sure to have a proof point at the ready. For instance, if a college admissions officer asks the athlete how he is a "goal-getter," he can support it with quantifiable goals he has set for himself academically, personally, and athletically. He can also share that he is the captain of the soccer team and president of the school's Model U.N. Club.

Now, let's go back to Peter to see what his Uniquely Me statement is: "My curious, creative, and analytical nature drives me to generate new ideas to solve complex scientific and math problems." Peter has ample proof of this: He spent last summer getting certificates in UX design and database management. Further, he is self-taught in Google Analytics. Peter also has AP classes in chemistry, physics, and calculus under his belt. And he launched and is spearheading an environmental club at his high school.

Before you share the Uniquely Me statement, you would, of course, introduce yourself and share some context based on the situation.

Okay, now it's your turn (with a running start):

Example: I'm Jessica Bowen. I'm currently a senior at XYZ high school and am interested in majoring in nutrition…

_____

_____

_____

_____

Your Uniquely Me statement should provide ample information and be delivered enthusiastically. Before you finalize your Uniquely Me statement, run through this checklist:

☐ Highlights my strengths

☐ Concise (one to two sentences; less than 25 words)

☐ Memorable

☐ Personal and authentic

Congratulations! You now have a grasp of your own competitive advantage, your audience, and a strong Uniquely Me statement. And take note: Your personal brand statement is a living, breathing entity. It evolves over time as you continue to learn more about yourself and what makes you unique in this world.

BRANDAMENTALS

And in the meantime, commit these top takeaways to memory:

1 **Self-awareness is all that.** Start by defining yourself. The stronger your grasp of your strengths, the stronger your personal brand. Take time to reflect.

2 **Conduct a self-audit.** Spend time mapping out your skills and your passions. Doing that will help you craft everything from your résumé to your college admission essay.

3 **Know your target audience.** Personal brands aren't *me-me-me*. They're also about others — the audience you're looking to impress. Determine who that is: College admission officers, recruiters, and so forth.

4 **Develop your "slogan."** Crystallize your uniqueness and why someone should choose your application for college admissions or a job opening. Create a concise blurb that highlights your best qualities. This is your "Uniquely Me" statement or elevator pitch — use it often.

PART II – THE FUTURE YOU

Discover Your Perfect Career Path

Understanding where you are coming *from* is invaluable as you think about where you are going *to*. That's where goals come in. Setting short- and long-term goals allows you to chart a course and develop a strategy for success. But remember: Goals can be flexible. As you learn more about yourself and the world around you, you — and your goals — should evolve.

As you envision what's ahead, the below activities will allow you to plan big and small. They will also help you connect your interests to your potential career and educational choices.

Exercise

Consider what you like to do in your leisure time or in school. Check the boxes that apply:

☐ Working with your hands (woodworking, painting, cooking, sewing)

☐ Science (lab work, research, astronomy, environment)

☐ Technology (app development, coding)

☐ Sports (athletics, coaching, sports management)

☐ Humanities (literature, history)

☐ Working with children (tutoring, babysitting)

☐ Math (solving complex problems, numbers games)

☐ Theater (acting, talent managing)

☐ Other:

_____

_____

_____

_____

Career Exploration Tips

How do you begin? Here are some tips to get you started:

• **Keep a passion list:** Journal a list of extracurricular activities, classes, and hobbies that spark passion. Don't censor your thoughts as you write — simply let them flow. As your list expands, you'll begin to recognize patterns among the types of things that attract you.

• **Review the last section and your Uniquely Me statement:** With this in hand, explore careers that match your skills and passion.

• **Take a career assessment to identify possible career choices.** These typically fall into two categories:

■ Career aptitude tests, which assess your strengths and weaknesses to help you determine a career path and college major.

■ Career interest tests, which identify career or college major pathways based on your likes and dislikes.

• **Engage in activities that may spark career interest,** such as academic clubs, debate teams, or the arts.

• **Get involved in a student organization that advances career readiness,** like SkillsUSA, DECA, or the Future Business Leaders of America. (See additional career readiness resources in the Entrepreneurial section on page 159)

• **Serve as a volunteer in your community.** See the "Doing Good" section for some volunteering ideas.

• **Cast a wide net.** Don't limit yourself to pursuing a career based on your college major. Think broadly about all the career paths that are open to you. Be open-minded, as there are endless career possibilities — and who knows what jobs will arise thanks to new technologies and markets?

• **Pay close attention to the rockstars in your desired industry.** Scour their online profiles, read their articles, follow their tweets, and watch what they wear and how they speak. You can learn a lot by studying the actions and attitudes of leaders.

• **Get in the know.** Set up free, online keyword news alerts for employers, industries, events, and people related to your industries of interest.

EXERCISE:
Time Travel to Meet Your Future Self

We all have dreams. Perhaps you want to be an actress or an engineer or a professional athlete. Or perhaps, you simply want to improve your public speaking or writing skills.

No matter the scope of your dreams, imagining your future is the first step toward realizing them. In the exercise that follows, allow your mind to wander and reflect on all the possibilities life offers. Don't limit yourself!

Let's get started: Imagine if you had a method to visit the future. Then, imagine if, while there, you ran into your FUTURE self…

What causes you to suddenly travel to the future? Was it a time machine? A dream? An accident? Use the space below to demonstrate what happened, utilizing images and words.

You have arrived 30 years into the future. How are you feeling? Are you sad, happy, nervous, or excited? What is your impression?

What happens when you meet your "future self"? What did you study in college? Did you achieve your career aspirations? What does your family look like? Does your "future self" have some advice for the present you?

Time to go home. How will you get back to the present day? What are your takeaways from this experience? Any parting advice from your future self?

The Informational Interview: A True Goldmine

Informational interviews are a great way to learn about potential careers, and they're quite simple. They're just conversations with professionals in various industries that align with your personality, interests, and skills. These interviews can open your eyes to careers you may not have considered before, and they're also a great way to get a head start on networking (and potentially unlock an internship or job opportunity down the road).

You might feel like you're imposing by asking an older professional for an informational interview. But remember: Most people love giving advice and sharing their knowledge.

What are the goals of an informational interview?
- To get a feeling for what a particular type of career is like and if you might enjoy it.
- To determine important details like job tasks and working conditions.
- To discover related careers you never knew existed.
- To determine academic requirements and related volunteer, seasonal, part-time, and internship opportunities.

Deciding who to interview:
- First, decide which career you want to explore.
- Then, meet with your career or guidance counselor to clarify interests, skills, and earning goals.
- Consider interviewing both those who are at the same level you will be when entering the workforce and more senior people.
- How to find these people:
  - Network with friends, family, and teachers.
  - Schools often have alumni databases with graduates who are open to being interviewed.
  - Contact businesses and organizations that hire the type of workers you would like to consult.
  - Attend high school job fairs.

Informational interview tips:

1. Do your homework. Your interviewee is doing you a favor, so come prepared. Research the person you are meeting, their company, and their industry. Check out their LinkedIn profile as well as the company website. If you come across something interesting from your research, it could be a great conversation starter.

2. Show up with good questions. Take full advantage of the interviewee's knowledge and ask open-ended questions about their industry experience, as well as the required educational background and skills for the particular career path. Be comfortable going "off script" when digging deeper into topics based on the direction of your conversation.

3 Take notes. This will demonstrate how much you value their knowledge and experience. Plus, you don't want to forget anything you learn.

4 Dress appropriately. Leave the ripped jeans behind and dress professionally. This may not be a job interview, but you still always want to make a good impression.

5 Pay attention to body language. The way you communicate with your body can be more revealing than the words that come out of your mouth. For example, body language can imply you are confident, bored, or nervous. Be sure to maintain eye contact, avoid slouching, and steer clear of fidgeting.

6 Express gratitude. Thank the interviewee for their time at the beginning and end of your conversation. And always be sure to email a short thank you message within 24 hours of the interview.

Informational interviews can be a goldmine for your career, providing essential guidance and valuable contacts. Since they're often short — just 15 to 30 minutes — be sure to maximize every moment.

Got writer's block ahead of your interview? Here are some questions to kickstart your conversation:

Career-related questions:
- How did you decide on your career path — what made you choose this field, why did you accept and leave positions?
- What classes, activities, or other parts of your college experience best prepared you for your career?
- What do you like best about this career?
- What are some of the more rewarding and challenging parts of your career?
- I really like doing _____. Are there opportunities to do this type of work in this career?
- What skills or personality traits does a person in this field need?
- What kind of growth opportunities does this career offer to entry-level employees?
- What is the future outlook for your industry?
- Are you willing to review my résumé and offer some advice?

Day-to-day-related questions:
- How did you find this job?
- What type of tasks do you spend the majority of your time on?
- Is your schedule flexible or set?
- Does your position require travel?

Training/Education-related questions:

- How did you prepare for this career?
- How should people interested in this career prepare themselves?
- Which entry-level jobs provide the most learning opportunities?
- What experience and skills are most impressive in your field?
  What is the best way to gain this experience?
- Are there any resources (e.g., books, online groups) that you suggest?

Dream quotes to inspire your life:

> *Follow Your Dreams, They Know The Way.*
>
> **— Kobi Yamada**

> *If You Can Dream It, You Can Do It.*
>
> *— Walt Disney*

> *We Have To Dream. How Else Will We Make A Future That Does Not Yet Exist?*
>
> *— Simon Sinek*

> *Whatever The Mind Can Conceive And Believe, It Can Achieve.*
>
> *— Napoleon Hill*

ACTIVITY:
Creating a Vision Board

Earlier, when you journeyed into the future, we envisioned what it would look and feel like to accomplish your goals. But time travel is a shortcut none of us actually have. And sticking to your goals one day at a time can be challenging.

Creating a vision board is one of the best ways to stay motivated and focused on your goals. The images on the board are representations of your goals and dreams and can provide regular inspiration.

To start the process, consider what gives you passion and purpose. Ask yourself: *If I had one year to live, what would I do? If money were not an issue, how would I spend the rest of my life?* While our focus in this book is on academic and career success, you should still include personal desires, like running the NYC marathon. It's essential to nurture both our professional and personal lives. To be successful in one area, you need to create success in the other.

> *Allow your passion to become your purpose, and it will one day become your profession.*
>
> — *Bestselling Author, Gabrielle Bernstein*

Now it's time to draw or gather relevant images, quotes, and words to create a collage. There are no rules or limits. Use a poster board and hang it up in your room highlighting all your aspirations!

While vision boards are a great tool, there are countless others for staying inspired, from journaling to meditation to listening to uplifting music. No matter what tools you pick, make sure to stay the course.

Goal-Setting Is a (Complicated) Science and an Art

What do successful people have in common, whether a marathon runner, valedictorian, or billionaire? They understand that setting effective goals is essential. Setting goals gives you a purpose and a sense of accomplishment when you reach them.

In our fast-paced world, we get caught up in day-to-day tasks. Goal-setting is key to success. If you want to achieve anything meaningful, you can't just sit around and hope for it to happen on its own. You need to manufacture your own opportunities.

But setting goals isn't as simple as jotting a few sentences down on paper. Indeed, goal-setting skills are a real muscle you need to develop — and the SMART approach can help.

What are SMART goals?

SMART (Specific, Measurable, Achievable, Relevant, and Time-Bound) is an acronym you can use to guide your goal-setting. It ensures the clarity, focus, and motivation you need to craft meaningful goals. Let's examine each of these characteristics individually.

SPECIFIC. It is important to be as clear as possible about what you wish to accomplish. An unclear goal will result in wasted efforts (e.g., *I want to make more money*). Goals should address who, what, when, where, and why. The narrower a goal, the more you'll be able to detail the steps necessary to achieve it.

MEASURABLE. How are you quantifying your goal? How will you prove you are making headway? Measurable goals allow you to track your progress. Setting milestones along the way will enable you to re-evaluate and course-correct as needed.

ACHIEVABLE. How realistic is it to attain your goal? First, clear actions or tasks need to be aligned with your goal. Setting goals you can accomplish within a specific time frame will help keep you motivated and focused.

RELEVANT. Each goal should align with your values and larger, long-term goals. Explore "the why" behind the goal. Why is this goal important to you? Is working toward this goal worthwhile? How will this help you contribute toward your long-term goals?

TIME-BOUND. What is your goal time frame? A completion date can help provide motivation and help you prioritize. Every goal should be assigned a deadline.

Below are a few example goals which are assessed using the SMART framework. In this case, the goal-setter is a college-bound high school senior.

GOAL: I will submit 12 applications to colleges by December 31 to ensure my acceptance to a school

Specific: This goal is clear and straightforward.
Measurable: Progress can be tracked as each application is submitted.
Achievable: With the majority of applications available via Common App, this is a realistic goal.
Relevant: College application deadlines typically fall between January and February of a student's senior year.
Time-bound: The deadline is December 31st.

GOAL: I will apply for six scholarships by February 1 to help cover college tuition

Specific: Once again, the goal is clear and straightforward.
Measurable: Progress can be tracked as each scholarship application is submitted.
Achievable: Applying for six scholarships is realistic with proper time management.
Relevant: This is a pertinent goal for most students, as higher education can be expensive.
Time-bound: The deadline is February 1st.

GOAL: I will launch a drop shipping business by June 1st, so I can be my own boss this summer and earn $10,000, with the first sale occurring by June 15th.

Specific: This goal clearly defines the type of business and quantifies revenue goals.
Measurable: Progress can be tracked by weekly or monthly sales revenues.
Achievable: Existing technology (e.g., Shopify) allows the student to set their business up quickly.
Relevant: Getting summer jobs is difficult, and the ability to start a company is rewarding.
Time-bound: The deadline to start the business is June 1, followed shortly by a clear sales goal.

Now it's your turn. In the exercise below, you will set your own SMART goals.

EXERCISE: Goal-Setting

Goal 1: Academic — What is one thing you desire to improve academically?

S _____

M _____

A _____

R _____

T _____

Goal 2: Personal — Do you want to start a fitness program, travel, or improve your public speaking skills?

S _____

M _____

A _____

R _____

T _____

Goal 3: Professional — What is your dream career?

S _____

M _____

A _____

R _____

T _____

Ready to take action? Now that you've completed the exercise, let's consider a few tips to achieve your goals.

Brand Up
SMART
GOALS
WORKSHEET

SPECIFIC

What exactly do I want to do?

MEASURABLE

How will I track my progress?

ATTAINABLE

Is this realistic for me?
Do I have what I need to make it possible?

RELEVANT

Why am I doing this? Does it matter to me?

TIME-ORIENTED

When will I have this completed?

Taking action to achieve your goals

It's not easy to set goals and figure out what we want in life. Achieving goals requires hard work and commitment. Your ability to follow through and do whatever is necessary is key. A mental game is involved — you have to **really** want it! Passion, purpose, and a burning desire will help you reach your goals. Keep these four essentials in mind:

- **Prioritize your goals:** If the goal is truly important to you, treat it as such. Schedule actions related to your goal before other unrelated tasks, and don't procrastinate. Make sure to record your goals in a journal, word document, or app.
- **Commitment:** When roadblocks arise to test your resolve, remind yourself why you set the goal in the first place. Revisit your goals worksheet to ensure you're staying on track and to get reenergized. Remind yourself it will all be worth it in the end.
- **Make it a habit.** You need to stop overthinking and simply DO it! Determine what routine works for you and then put it into practice. Maintain a constant drumbeat of activity that supports your goals in your everyday life.
- **Maintain flexibility:** It's inevitable: You *will* be thrown a curveball, and the routines and habits you've formed *will* get messed up. This is where flexibility is critical — find ways to pursue your goals even as unexpected things happen with relationships, health, or finances.

You may think that goal-setting is all about planning for the future. But in reality, it's also important to take a moment to reflect on your progress. Celebrating our accomplishments is a great way to stay motivated and push ourselves to reach our goals. So don't forget to celebrate your wins along the way!

"This is not a typo: "To Do" is too passive, so I prefer to call it a "Must Do" list. Ask yourself: *What must I do today to support my purpose and goals? How does this activity help my purpose?* Clear goals and Must Dos are critical to transforming desire into reality and overcoming obstacles, distractions, and burnout."

"MUST DO" LIST

Mindset

What does mindset have to do with goal-setting and achievement? Everything!

A mindset is a set of beliefs that shape how you feel, think, and act. And it greatly impacts your success or failure. Indeed, your mindset is key to realizing short and long-term academic and career goals. Mindset also plays a crucial role in how you cope with life's challenges.

Don't believe me? According to Dr. Carol Dweck, Stanford psychologist and bestselling author of *Mindset: The New Psychology of Success: How We Can Learn to Fulfill Our Potential*, mindset does indeed play a significant role in determining achievement and success. Dweck is renowned for her research in human motivation and theory of fixed mindset vs. growth mindset.

Whereas a growth mindset empowers ambitious beliefs, a fixed mindset imposes self-limiting beliefs, which can hinder achieving goals. Students with a growth mindset believe they can develop their talents and intelligence through learning and effort. They have an optimistic, can-do attitude and believe that hard work and practice lead to mastery. On the contrary, those with a fixed mindset believe that their talents and abilities are set in stone no matter how much effort they exert. They view success in life as primarily determined by the skills a person is born with. If you have a fixed mindset, you believe you lack the skills to accomplish certain goals. With a growth mindset, you believe anything is possible and that it just requires stepping out of your comfort zone.

Growth vs. fixed mindset is not an either/or thing. Dweck's studies show that approximately 40 percent of U.S. students display a growth mindset and 40 percent a fixed mindset, while the remaining 20 percent show mixed profiles. Research shows that students with a growth mindset tend to do better in academics, enjoy education more, participate more frequently in class, and have more positive aspirations for their future.

When students undertake an intervention to move from a fixed to a growth mindset, they immediately start performing at higher levels in school.

The following attitudes characterize a fixed mindset and growth mindset:

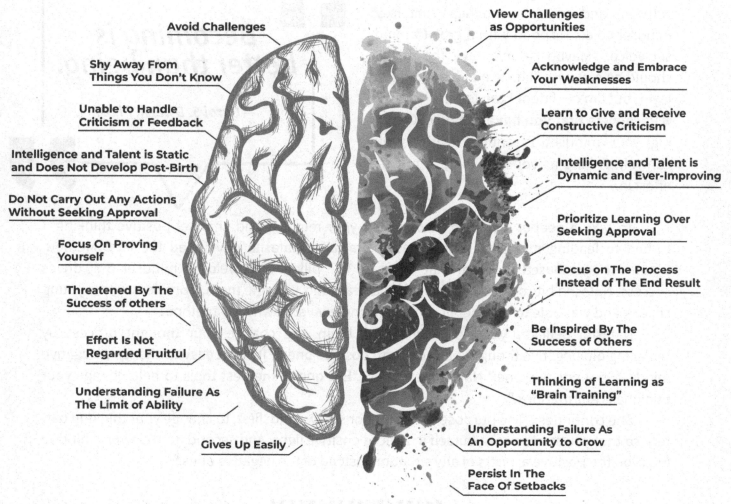

Avoid Challenges

Shy Away From
Things You Don't Know

Unable to Handle
Criticism or Feedback

Intelligence and Talent is Static
and Does Not Develop Post-Birth

Do Not Carry Out Any Actions
Without Seeking Approval

Focus On Proving
Yourself

Threatened By The
Success of others

Effort Is Not
Regarded Fruitful

Understanding Failure As
The Limit of Ability

Gives Up Easily

View Challenges
as Opportunities

Acknowledge and Embrace
Your Weaknesses

Learn to Give and Receive
Constructive Criticism

Intelligence and Talent is
Dynamic and Ever-Improving

Prioritize Learning Over
Seeking Approval

Focus on The Process
Instead of The End Result

Be Inspired By The
Success of Others

Thinking of Learning as
"Brain Training"

Understanding Failure As
An Opportunity to Grow

Persist In The
Face Of Setbacks

How to unfix a fixed mindset

According to Dweck, you can change from a fixed to a growth mindset. Here are some strategies from the *Mindset* book:

- **Focus on learning over achievement.** With a fixed mindset, you are focused solely on the outcome and miss out on the learning moments along the way. Instead, learn to enjoy the journey despite setbacks. Experience and personal growth can be more valuable than "winning." Your dream school may decline your admission, or the internship you were hoping for may fall through. Expect failure; there are lessons to be learned. And remember, each failure is a stepping stone toward success.

- **Pay attention to your words and thoughts.** Be conscious of how you speak to yourself (and others). Replace negative thoughts with more positive ones to build a growth mindset. When a fixed mindset takes hold, incorporate "yet" at the end of the sentence, which signals that you can overcome any struggles. For instance, rather than saying, "I can't learn a foreign language," replace it with, "I haven't mastered a foreign language yet." Similarly, imagine you hear about a coveted internship position. A student with a fixed mindset thinks, "That internship position is out of my league." Instead, that student should think, "The internship position is challenging. I'm going for it."

■ **Take on challenges.** Embrace challenges rather than avoiding them. When you face setbacks and criticism and hear that fixed mindset voice, respond with a growth mindset voice. "Maybe I don't have the talent" should be met with "I have no idea how to do it yet, but I'm confident I can learn."

■ **Recognize that you have a choice.** Changing your mindset is entirely within your control, as long as you're willing to put the effort in.

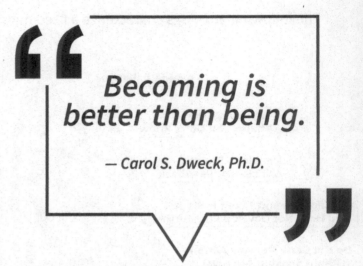

> *Becoming is better than being.*
>
> — *Carol S. Dweck, Ph.D.*

To take a deeper dive into how to shift your mindset and channel positive thinking, I turned to leading mindset coach Natasha Graziano. Natasha developed the MBS Method, a neuroscience-based program that relies on five pillars to develop a mindset that drives success. Natasha hit rock bottom herself five years ago — single mom, homeless with a young child — and was able to turn her life around using her very own MBS method.

Natasha believes you can rewire your brain and change your thought process by replacing old negative thought patterns with positive ones. "It is not easy to change a negative mindset to a positive one," Natasha explains. "But one of the best tools to help change your thinking is affirmations."

She continues: "The purpose of affirmations is twofold: first, to change your thinking pattern so that you start to see yourself in a more positive light. And second, to train your mind to focus on the positive aspects of any situation instead of the negative ones."

■■■■■■■■■■■■■■■■■■■

What are affirmations exactly? Affirmations are positive statements that can help you challenge and overcome negative thoughts. For example: "I am strong." I use affirmations to ace new business opportunities, grow my agency, and empower my team. Affirmations are not magic; they must be accompanied by hard, smart work. But they can still go a long way. Don't just take my word for it. Some of the most successful individuals — including Arianna Huffington, Oprah Winfrey, and LinkedIn CEO Jeff Weiner — claim that affirmations have played a significant part in their success.

Now, use thoughts and words from your goal-setting activity (page 59) to write five affirmation statements. For some inspiration, consider these:

- My potential to succeed is limitless.
- I am a success in all that I do.
- My life is a gift, and I'm grateful for everything I have.
- I'm open to new adventures in my life.
- I am thankful for my family and friends.
- My needs and wants are important.
- I'm worthy of love.
- I act with courage and confidence.

Now it's your turn:

1. _____

2. _____

3. _____

4. _____

5. _____

Make sure to repeat these to yourself often and with confidence!

Personal Learning Networks (PLNs)

What is a PLN?

A personal learning network, or PLN, originates from the connectivism theory by George Siemens. According to Siemens, "Connectivism is a learning theory for the Digital Age" to which the "starting point of learning is the individual who feeds information into the network, which feeds information back to individuals who in turn feed information back into the network as part of a cycle" (Siemens, 2004).

That may all sound complicated — but it's not. In its simplest terms, a PLN is a group of like-minded people who learn together. It could be classmates who study together or members of a LinkedIn group. PLNs provide an opportunity to mutually share your knowledge and experience. PLNs can be both online and offline, but for purposes of this discussion, we will focus on the online.

Here are three defining features of a PLN:

■ PLNs are developed largely through the use of social media, such as Twitter, LinkedIn, YouTube, Facebook, and blogs. Developing a PLN requires you to follow individuals, businesses, and nonprofits you aspire to learn from. Sharing your own experience and knowledge is not mandatory, but it is recommended. And, of course, engaging through commenting, tagging, and sharing is beneficial.

■ The purpose of a PLN is **personalized learning**. Once you determine your goals, you can acquire the sources necessary to address them by tapping into a broad base of knowledge and expertise. Topics of exploration can range from marketing to pizza-making to technology. It's your choice.

■ The power of PLNs comes from connecting with others who have similar interests, ideas, or resources.

Why a PLN? It's worth the investment: Still not sold on the idea of a PLN? Here are four reasons to participate:

■ **Take charge of your professional development:** PLNs take you beyond classroom learning, expanding your knowledge and skills on various topics. This ensures you can outclass the competition.

■ **Depth and breadth of experience:** PLNs provide a well-rounded, 24/7 global network for professional and personal development. You can't find that anywhere else.

■ **Form valuable connections:** When you participate in a PLN, you're also networking. Building these meaningful relationships will give you an edge in your early career, open doors to internship or job opportunities, and even ignite your creativity.

■ **Stay up to date:** Given the speed at which the online world moves, it can be difficult to remain up to date on any given topic or industry. PLNs can help with that, ensuring you're always learning and communicating with other experts.

Quick tips for building a PLN:

1 **Determine your focus:** Whether it's the downtown basketball court or the stage in your local community, identify what motivates and interests you from both an academic and career perspective.

2 **Learn from others:** Who inspires you? Research relevant experts online. The possibilities are endless: blogs, RSS feeds, email lists, websites, videos, and podcasts can provide a steady stream of up-to-date information on an athlete, actor, or other professional you admire. Tap into their expertise and then their network to uncover even more experts.

3 **Share what you learn:** Don't be selfish. Give back to your PLN, too. Use social networks to retweet others and leave meaningful and thought-provoking comments on blog posts that you find interesting. Join chat rooms and discussion forums and share in professional dialogues. Let your voice be heard by creating and sharing original content on a specific topic. Consider creating your very own blog or YouTube channel.

Now, let's put all this into action. Following, find suggested PLNs for several potential career paths (STEM, business, and liberal arts). The sources provided will give you a good foundation for career exploration. Lastly, curate your PLN by adding (or deleting) subject matter experts and resources to make it your own.

Personal Learning Networks By Category

STEM

This category includes, but is not limited to science, technology, engineering, and math.

STEM Topics	Facebook	Twitter	Instagram
Science	National Geographic Green Energy News Climate Desk Green Living The Ecologist National Wildlife Federation Climate Nexus	National Geographic Green Energy News Climate Desk Green Living Digg Nature The Ecologist National Wildlife Federation Carbon Explorer Climate Nexus	Scott Kelly Brian Cox Dr. Karl Kruszelnicki Phil Torres Athena Brensberger Neil Harbisson Bipolaire61 Popular Science NASA Goddard David Doubilet Natalie Panek Dianna Cowern Pardis Sabeti Mitchell Moffit Abigail Harrison Georgia Aquarium The Bronx Zoo Liberty Science Center

STEM Topics	Facebook	Twitter	Instagram
Technology	Mashable Gizmodo Techcrunch Wired Read Write Stratechery CNN Tech CNET News Venture Beat WSJ D Note to Self Om Malik Nick Bilton DataGenetics	Mashable Gizmodo Techcrunch Wired Read Write Stratechery Marketplace Tech CNN Tech CNET News Venture Beat WSJ D Note to Self Om Malik Nick Bilton Facebook AI DataGenetics HackADay Machine Learning Andrew Ng Yann LeCun Partnership on AI PyTorch TensorFlow Big Data Revolution	Tech by Guff TechCrunch Christian Sanz-Skycatch Technology Mogul Thingverse Bane Tech Jose Ramos Marques Brownlee Alexis Ohanian

Engineering	MITEngineering
	Engineering Science
	DARPA
	Stanford Engineering
	Engineeringcom
	IEEE Spectrum
	National Science
	Foundation
	MIT
	DIY Drones
		MITEngineering
		Engineering Science
		DARPA
		Stanford Engineering
		Engineeringcom
		IEEE Spectrum
		Matt Anderson
		Engineering
		Thingverse
		Engineer Update
		David Rush
		SpaceX
		Chris Anderson
		DIY Drones
			Interesting Engineering
			Wyss Institute
			The Art Department of
			  Popular Science Magazine
			Harvard University's
			  Science in the News
			Futurism
			CERN

STEM Topics	Facebook	Twitter	Instagram
Math	Desmos	Desmos	Kacie Travis
	Wolfram	Wolfram	Mathgiraffe
	Wolfram Alpha	Wolfram Alpha	8thgrademathteacher
	FiveThirtyEight	FiveThirtyEight	Ms. Boyers Cabin
	Numberphile	Numberphile	Divid3andconquer
	National Math and Science	National Math and Science	Smithcurriculumconsulting
	UK Mathematics Trust	UK Mathematics Trust	Theunhelpfulteacher
	DataGenetics	DataGenetics	Paul Salomon
	FiveThirtyEight	Alex Bellows	Nat Banting
	Pew Research	Matt Parker	Kate Nowak
	Chartsbin	FiveThirtyEight	Card Colm Mulcahy
		Pew Research	Marcus du Sautoy
		Gallup	Peter Rowlett
		Gallup Analytics	Ivars Peterson
		Chartsbin	Matt Enlow
		Max Roser	Colin Wright
		Flowing Data	
		Simply Statistics	
		Stats & Data Science	

STEM Topics	YouTube	Podcasts
Science	Vsauce	Minuteearth
	AsapSCIENCE	Sierra Club
	SmarterEveryDay	The Elephant
	Kurzgesagt	Warm Regards
	SciShow	Climate History Podcast
	Veritasium	Radio EcoShock
	Minute Physics	Climate One
	It's Okay To Be Smart	America Adapts
	Periodic Videos	
	Home Science	

STEM Topics	YouTube	Podcasts
Technology	Google Tech Talks Make MIT CSAIL Wired This Week In Tech The Verge Geeks Life UnBox therapy CNET TV Austin Evans Marques Brownlee Linus Tech Tips Newegg Studios Mashable Gizmodo Techcrunch Wired	Pivot The Vergecast All Tech is Human In Machines We Trust Exponential View Your Undivided Attention Internet Explorer Radical AI Podcast This Week in Tech Code Breaker
Engineering	Stanford Intro to Robotics Robotics with Python Raspberry Pi and GoPiGo NPTEL SparkFun Electronics Engineering Learning Robotics and Electronics class Make a Line Following Robot Motherboard CS50 The New Boston Computer History Eli the Computer Guy Computerphile MySQL Tutorial MIT Machine Learning Course NIPS AI Courses Alex Smola Alexander Ilher MITEngineering MIT SpaceX	99% Invisible Level-up Engineering Engineering Commons Engineering Career Coach The Amp Hour Electronics Engines of Our Ingenuity Curiosity Daily Engineering Reimagined If You Were An Engineer Teach The Geek The Undistilled Series Cliff Notes Podcast The Structural Engineering Channel Designed for life The STEMusic Podcast In Machines We Trust Create the Future Podcast (Queen Elizabeth Prize) Twenty Days STEM Sessions

STEM Topics	YouTube	Podcasts
Math	Khan Academy 3Blue1Brown VSauce2 Numberphile Brightstorm Wow Math Patrick JMT Statistics Learning Centre National Programme on Technology Enhanced Learning Pew Research	My Favourite Theorem The Secrets of Mathematics A Brief History of Mathematics Math ED Podcast Breaking Math Three brown one blue In our time — mathematics Relatively Prime The Women in Math: The Limit Doesn't Exist Mathematical Moments from the American Mathematical Society

BUSINESS/ENTREPRENEURSHIP

This category includes, but is not limited to students interested in pursuing finance, marketing, operations, human resources, and sales.

Business/ Entrepreneurship Topics	Facebook	Twitter	Instagram
Business & Finance	Wall St. Journal Business Insider Fast Company Forbes Market Watch Dealbook The Economist SquawkBox Financial Times Harvard Business Review Stock Twits Priceconomics Jim Cramer Financial Samurai	Wall St. Journal Business Insider Fast Company Forbes Reuters Business Market Watch Dealbook The Economist SquawkBox Financial Times Stock Twits NY Times Business Priceconomics ECB Federal Reserve Jim Cramer Pedro de Costa Nouriel Roubini Financial Samurai Paul Krugman Andrew Ross Sorkin WSJ Real Time Economics Harvard Business Review	Bae on a Budget Beworth Finance Modern Frugality POHVenture Tyler McBroom White Coat Investor Go Fund Yourself Clevergirlfinance My Frugal Year Moneytothemasses Good Money Girl Money Medics Thisgirltalksmoney Rainchq The Financial Diet Thrifty Londoner Mr MoneyJar Activebudgeter Wise Woman Wallet

Business/ Entrepreneurship Topics	Facebook	Twitter	Instagram
Entrepreneurship & Venture Capital	Inc Kickstarter Re/code Tim Ferriss Techstars Venturebeat Bizprivy Entrepreneur Jonah Peretti	Inc Kickstarter Re/code Fred Wilson Jordan Cooper Tim Ferriss Benedict Evans Techstars Venturebeat Bizprivy Mark & Dave Brevedy Rob Go Entrepreneur Chris Dixon Andy Weissman John Borthwick Jonah Peretti Kanyi Maqubela Vinod Khosla	500 startups 1776 VC Istrategylabs Everette Taylor Peter Voogd Marie Forleo Gary Vaynerchuck 6amsuccess Natalie Franke Shane Feldman Amber Lilyestrom Melyssa Griffin Sir Richard Branson Justin Dry Harvard Business Review
Advertising & Marketing	Adweek Ad Age Marketing Magazine Marketing Cloud HubSpot CMO.com Seer Interactive Salesforce Michael Stelzner Gary Vee Simon Mainwaring Jay Baer Lilach Bullock	Adweek Ad Age Marketing Magazine Marketing Cloud HubSpot CMO.com Seer Interactive Salesforce Michael Stelzner Gary Vee Simon Mainwaring Burt Steingraeber Jay Baer Lilach Bullock	Ad Week NoGood HubSpot 2PM Inc Marketing Humor Digital Marketer Design4Growth Canva Marketing 360 Sprout Social LaterMedia Digital Chadvertising DTC Newsletter Dain Walker Unemployed Marketers

Business/Entrepreneurship Topics	YouTube	Podcasts
Business & Finance	Wall St. Journal Business Insider Fast Company Forbes The Economist Financial Times Harvard Business Review ECB Bloomberg World Economic Forum eHow Finance Freakonomics The Street The Motley Fool Reggie Middleton Zachs Investment Research Morningstar Michael Stelzner Gary Vee	The Economist: All Audio NPR's Planet Money Marketplace Slate Money Freakonomics So Money Bloomberg Surveillance CNBC Fast Money HBR IdeaCast
Entrepreneurship & Venture Capital	Entrepreneur Mag Inc Fast Company Y Combinator Noah Kagan Roberto Blake GaryVee HubSpot	How I Built This Startup Traction How to Start a Startup Eventual Millionaire This week in Startups Entrepreneur on File

Business/ Entrepreneurship Topics	YouTube	Podcasts
Advertising & Marketing	Pat Flynn Ahrefs Brian Dean Noah Kagan Vanessa Lau Gary Vaynerchuk WPCrafter Social Media Examiner vidIQ Semrush Income School AppSumo HubSpot Neil Patel	Beancast Marketing podcast Six Pixels of Separation Marketing over Coffee Call to Action Growth Byte Power to the Small Business #AskGaryVee Marketing Update AdAge Outlook Social Zoom Factor Perpetual Traffic Mike Gingerich's Halftime Mike Podcast

LIBERAL ARTS

This category includes, but is not limited to students interested in pursuing English, history, philosophy, foreign languages, and communications.

Liberal Arts Topics	Facebook	Twitter	Instagram

English	Poetry Foundation
	Poetry Society
	NY Review of Books
	Goodreads
	Open Culture
	Brain Pickings
	Mental Floss
	Arts & Letters Daily
	Interesting
	  Literature
	AmLit in the World
	Lit Lovers
	The Author's Guild
	Writer's Digest
	Grammar Girl
		Poetry Foundation
		Poetry Society
		NY Review of Books
		Guardian Books
		Goodreads
		Open Culture
		Brain Pickings
		Mental Floss
		Arts & Letters Daily
		Lit lovers
		Interesting Literature
		Malcolm Gladwell
		AmLit in the World
		Joanna Penn
		The Author's Guild
		Daily Writing Tips
		Chuck Sambuchino
		Jane Friedman
		Jennie Nash
		Writer's Digest
		Grammar Girl
		Madam Grammar
		Henry David
		  Thoreau's Journal
		Bremner Editing Center
			James Trevino
			Elizabeth Sagan
			Jacquelin Firkins
			Joan Wong
			Rupi Kaur
			Kimberly Glyder
			Joan Wong
			Book Riot
			Library Journal
			Reese's Book Club
			Liz Alva
			Book of the Month
			Goodreads
			Pretty Book Places
			Kirkus Reviews
			Jenny Han
			Epic Reads
			Ice Cream Books
			American Booksellers
			  Association
			The Good Literary Agency
			The Last Bookstore

Liberal Arts Topics	Facebook	Twitter	Instagram
History	Library of Congress US National Archives Today's Document Smithsonian Institution National Museum of American History Civil War 150 NY Times Disunion Civil War National History Day Williamsburg for Teachers Edutopia	Weird History OER Project US National Archives USNA Today's Document Today in History Gilder Lehrman Inst. American Assoc. Of Historians Stanford History Education Group Zinn ed. Project Bruce Carlson Mary Beard Michael Beschloss The History Guy (Dan Snow) James Thorne Henry Louis Gates Jr. Matthew Ward Will Dalrymple	American Museum of Natural History The History Channel History Photographed MoMA AmericanCivilWar DaybyDay
Philosophy	Philosophy News Open Culture Brain Pickings Philosophy Now The School of Life Partially Examined Wireless Philosophy Daily Nous Philosophy Matters Philosophy Talk History of Philosophy	Philosophy News Open Culture Brain Pickings Philosopher's Eye Philosophy Now Alain de Botton The School of Life Only Philosophy Partially Examined Nigel Warburton Plato on Book Tour Peter Singer Oxford Philosophy Wireless Philosophy Ian Dyball Gregg Caruso Steven Pinker Why Philosophy Matters Philosophy Matters Philosophy Talk Brian Earp A Philosopher's Take Peter Boghossian History of Philosophy	Amanda Torroni Cleo Wade Briana Madia Christopher Poindexter Youareluminous Moonomens Heidiroserobbins Thehoodwitch

Liberal Arts Topics	Facebook	Twitter	Instagram
Psychology	Psychology Today National Institute of Mental Health PsyPost Psych News Scientific American Mind Psych Central Psych Science Learning and the Brain Neuroscience News PLOS neuro community All in the mind Paul Ekman	Psychology Today National Institute of Mental Health PsyPost Psych News Scientific American Mind Psychology Now Psych Central Psych Science Learning and the Brain Neuroskeptic Neuroscience News PLOS neuro community Soc Psych Update All in the mind Deborah Serani Dr. David Ballard Paul Ekman	Dr. Nicole LePera Sara Kuburić Nedra Glover Tawwab Vienna Pharaon Lisa Olivera Sarah Crosby Allyson Dinneen Whitney Hawkins Goodman Psychology Today Sara Kuburić Talkspace Lisaliveratherapy Theangrytherapist Notesfromyourtherapist Therapyforblackgirls Theanxietyhealer Themindgeek Minaa_b
Foreign Languages	AIIC Project to Help Interpreters in Conflict Zones American Translators Association Babelistas – volunteer interpreters and translators ELIA European Parliament interpreters – DG INTE Freelance Translators Glossarissimo	RosettaStone Aboutworldlangs LanguageJobs LanguageLog LanguageMastery World Language Classroom Meredith White A.C. Quinters Maris Hawkins	Sabe.languages Ohlalafrenchcourse speakFrenchlikeaboss LearnChineseDaily Hello_chineasy rodogaa Languagesmeme Nas.alive speakflex Instaideogram UnAutreCompte TalkinFrench French Words La francais ensemble French_add Paris Carte Postale Howtospanish Lea__english Michelle.languages languagesssss

Liberal Arts Topics	Facebook	Twitter	Instagram
Communications	Associated Press New York Times Washington Post Vox The Atlantic Time ProPublica NPR Newsweek Salon The Weekly Standard Slate National Review BuzzFeed News The New Yorker The Daily Beast The Upshot Poynter NPR's On the Media Neiman Lab Muck Rack Media Matters Media Diversified The Media is Dying Mediabistro Investigative Journalism Center for Investigative Reporting Longreads Mashable Social Media Social Media Today Mari Smith Darren Rowse Sean Gardner Customer Magnetism	Associated Press New York Times Washington Post Vox The Atlantic Time ProPublica NPR Newsweek Salon The Weekly Standard Slate National Review BuzzFeed News The New Yorker The Daily Beast The Upshot Poynter NPR's On the Media Neiman Lab Muck Rack Media Matters Media Diversified The Media is Dying Mediabistro Disrupt Media Lab Press Freedom Brian Stelter Jay Rosen Emily Bell Investigative Journalism Center for Investigative Reporting Longreads Social Media Insider Social Media Mind Mashable Social Media Social Media Today Steve Farnsworth Jeff Bullas Mari Smith Darren Rowse Sean Gardner Ted Coine Customer Magnetism	Adweek Eva Chen Josh Ostrovsky Iboommedia Business Insider Sue ZImmerman Richard Branson PRnews 360i Mediabistro Mashabe PRSA Ogilvy & Mather Edelman PR Golin Harris PR News Online Hootsuite Nitrogram Charity: Water National Geographic Go Pro Barack Obama Purple PR Exposure London Edelman Ketchum W Communications Weber Shandwick Iris Worldwide Burson-Marsteller M&C Saatchi Sport & Entertainment Hope & Glory M&C Satchi PR

Congratulations: You did it!

You've put in hard work reflecting on your past, examining the person you are today, and imagining your future. What you have discovered will ultimately become the essence and value of your personal brand. However, the work is far from done. Perhaps the most challenging aspect of developing a personal brand is determining how to use it. Now it is time for you to package up what makes you different and start broadcasting it. Let's get started and jump into the Development stage.

BRANDAMENTALS

Here are some top takeaways to keep top of mind:

1 **Take goal-setting seriously.** Setting goals takes practice. Make sure each one you set your mind to is the right balance of ambitious and achievable.

2 **Prioritize informational interviews.** Discussions with professionals in your intended field can be illuminating — and open the door for future internships and jobs.

3 **Get in the right mindset.** To succeed, you need a growth mindset — an optimistic, open-minded way of viewing the world.

4 **Tap into personal learning networks (PLNs).** PLNs can be simple, like a group of like-minded people on Twitter who share ideas. But they can also be incredibly powerful, providing deep knowledge and networking.

SECTION B:
DEVELOPMENT

PART III – STAYING ON MESSAGE

Good news: The Discovery stage — which is the most difficult part of building a personal brand — is complete. You've built a strong foundation. You are self-aware, you understand your audience, and you mastered your Uniquely Me statement. You looked into the future, did career exploration, set SMART goals, and learned the importance of mindset.

Now, welcome to the Development stage, where we tell your story in a variety of formats, online and off. And while these formats can be quite different, one thing must always remain the same: Your story must be compelling.

Why? Let's face it: American attention spans are declining. Today's average attention span is eight seconds, compared to 12 seconds in 2000. That's a 33 percent dip. Let's take this a step further: Since the average American speaks 140 words per minute, we now need to get our point across in just 20 words. You need to be a master of first impressions.

What's the best way to cut through the noise? With a compelling story! In this section, you will develop a handful of key messages customized for specific audiences. These messages can then be deployed across platforms, from LinkedIn bios to tweets to college admissions interviews. The good news is that learning how to craft key messages effectively will serve you for life. Strong messaging allows you to make a successful pitch, ace the interview, deliver a stunning keynote, or grow your social media following.

It's All About the Message

Starting the college application or job interview process can be overwhelming — even more so if you're not equipped with the right messaging. Key messages act as a foundation for all future communications and are the main points of information you want your audience to hear, understand, and remember. They are short, sweet summaries that clearly articulate what you do, why you do it, what makes you unique, and what value you bring to others.

Anatomy of a Strong Key Message

Key messages should be:
- **Strategic:** Before jumping into the weeds, be sure to engage in big-picture thinking. What are your visions, goals, values, and focus? Review the Uniquely Me statement you created on page 47 for inspiration.
- **Concise:** Make every word count and get to the point quickly. Strong messages are also short ones: just six to eight words per key message and four to five key messages total.

- **Consistent:** It is essential to be consistent with messaging across all communications, whether online or off, written or spoken.
- **Relevant:** You need to get inside the mindset of your target audience and understand "What's in it for them?" Shape what you need to communicate based on what's important to your audience.
- **Simple:** Use straightforward, easy-to-understand language, not jargon and acronyms.
- Memorable: Messages need to make a lasting impression. Ensure that messages are easy to recall and repeat.
- **Compelling:** Mix in at least one "wow" message that makes you **stand out** and is attention-grabbing.
- **Positive:** Use the active voice instead of the passive voice to demonstrate confidence.

Know your audience

Just as important as nailing the messaging? Understanding exactly who you're speaking to — that is, your audience. You should tailor messages to each particular audience. For example, an athletic coach, a summer internship, and an admissions officer. Ask yourself: What is important to each respective audience? When defining your target audience, consider their age, geography, and experience. The more narrowly defined your target audience, the greater the chance your messaging will resonate with them. If you define your audience too broadly, the message will likely be impersonal and read as boilerplate.

EXERCISE: How to Build a House Made Out of Messages

It's time to put pen to paper. But where to start? A great way to structure your messages is through a message house.

The roof of your message house is your **Uniquely Me statement** (also referred to as "**headline**" or "**umbrella statement**") that you established in the Discovery section. The statement links together all your key messages and is the main takeaway for your audience.

The pillars of your house are the **key messages**. They are the who, what, why, where, when, and how of your Uniquely Me statement. Keep your own goals and your audiences' goals in mind as you write.

Lastly, consider tone. It might be authoritative, technical, strong, trustworthy, or whimsical, depending on the audience. Of course, body language matters, too, when delivering these messages, whether facial expressions, posture, gestures, and eye movement. This comes into play during in-person or online interviews.

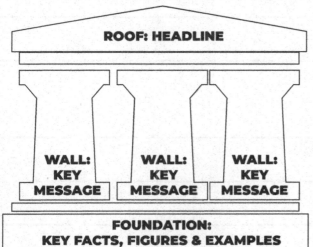

ROOF: HEADLINE

WALL: KEY MESSAGE

WALL: KEY MESSAGE

WALL: KEY MESSAGE

FOUNDATION: KEY FACTS, FIGURES & EXAMPLES

One more step and your house will be complete: **proof points** or **supporting statements.** This is the foundation of your house — the data that backs up your key messages. Substantiate all your points with concrete facts and figures to validate, distinguish, and add further credibility to what you're saying.

Let's get to work:

Uniquely Me Statement (repeat from page 47):

_____

_____

_____

ACTIVITY: Who is your audience? Select an audience (e.g., admissions officer, employer, athletic coach). Then, list four to five key messages with points that support your claim for that specific audience.

AUDIENCE #1:
_____

Key Messages: Proof Points

_____

_____

_____

_____

AUDIENCE #2:
_____

_____

_____

SAMPLE

AUDIENCE #1: College Admission officers

Key Message:	Proof Points:
"I'm a well-rounded student who wants to put my leadership skills to use in your sports management program."	Football team captain; 25-win milestone President, Model UN Club Leadership certificate 3.7 GPA

AUDIENCE #2: Athletic Coach

Key Message:	Proof Points:
"I'm a dedicated athlete and team player who motivates others to do their best."	Team captain 2020–22 Led team to 25-win milestone Gatorade Athlete of the Year, 2021

AUDIENCE #3: Prospective Employer

Key Message:	Proof Points:
"I'm a a self-starter with a strong work ethic and like to come up with new ideas to streamline processes."	Started own landscaping business as a high school senior Created new system to improve workflow efficiencies

Don't forget the maintenance

Just like a house, key messages need upkeep. Without it, they grow outdated — or start to crumble. Regularly review and update your key messages to ensure that they are relevant to your latest target audience. And remember to be consistent: If you're updating your key messaging in one place, update them in *all* places. It's also prudent to determine if your audience's needs have changed over time and adapt accordingly.

Messaging and the College Interview/Talking Points Exercise

Using your key messages, you can drive the narrative of any conversation. Remember: At its core, communication is about emphasizing and delivering the most relevant points. Below, find commonly asked questions, broken into five categories. Think about how you can use your key messages in response:

- **Interest in school:** What led you to apply to our school? Do you have a major(s) you'd like to pursue? What classes and activities are exciting to you? What will you contribute to the college?
- **High school experience:** What are your academic interests? What is your favorite subject(s)? What was your most challenging class in high school? What did you enjoy most about your high school experience? What was the most valuable extracurricular you participated in during high school?
- **Achievements:** What is your proudest achievement?
- **Extracurriculars:** What are you passionate about? What do you enjoy doing for fun?
- **The future you:** Where do you see yourself in the next ten years?

In addition to drawing on your message house to answer these, have some colorful anecdotes prepared, too. For example, maybe you established a high school environmental club. Or, perhaps you arranged for your choir to visit a local assisted living facility each month.

The prompts below can help to come up with colorful anecdotes:

Your proudest moment

_____

_____

Your favorite memories

_____

_____

Your biggest challenges

_____

_____

Times you overcame adversity

_____

_____

People you admire

_____

_____

New experiences you want to have in college

_____

_____

Can't-Miss College Interview Tips

Before we move on to the next section, here are some additional tips for the college interview:

■ **Visit in person:** If given the opportunity, nothing beats an in-person interview. Showing up shows you care.

■ **Do your homework:** Research the school and come prepared. Assemble examples of why you find the school appealing. And review your college application and essay to ensure consistency.

■ **Present your best self:** Dress neatly and conservatively. Shake the interviewer's hand before and after the interview. Talk naturally and show your enthusiasm and energy. Answer as decisively and positively as you can. Remember, the interviewer wants to get to know the personality _behind_ the ACTs, grades, and essays.

■ **Be curious:** An interview is a two-way process — the admissions officer expects you to ask (great) questions, too. Beforehand, craft a handful of meaningful questions that showcase your interest in the school. For example: "What kinds of students thrive here?" "Can you tell me about the alumni network?" and "How does the engineering program compare with other institutions?"

The All-Important Thank You Letter

You know your strengths. You know how to communicate them through key messages. And you've rehearsed your interview questions in front of the mirror. Now, it's time to get the ball rolling — to start sending those applications, typing those emails, and scheduling those in-person interviews.

As you write each correspondence, make sure you're weaving in your messages often and early. These are the common threads through your thank-you letters, cover letters, and other materials.

It's wise to assemble a file of customizable templates so that you can send out these items reliably and promptly. Below, you will find a series of templates that can be adapted to your specific situation. _Adapted_ is the keyword here: admission officers can sniff a template miles away, so personalization is a must.

Sample thank you letter: The thank you letter should be sent within 24 hours following the interview. Be sure to express gratitude, reinforce your interest in the school, and, once again, stress the unique value you bring to the campus. The letter should be brief — just two to three paragraphs — and carefully spell-checked. An excellent way to accomplish personalization is to include a shared interest uncovered during the interview. It is acceptable to email the thank you letter, but you may also want to consider sending a handwritten note. Here's an example:

DATE
Name/Title of Admissions Representative
Name of College
College Address
City, State, Zip Code

Dear Ms./Mrs. XYZ:

I enjoyed meeting with you earlier today and appreciate your time and insights. Our conversation further solidified my desire to attend University ABC. What draws me most to University ABC is your School of International Studies. The breadth and depth of the curriculum and study abroad program are impressive. As mentioned, I'm seeking to learn about different cultures, and your diverse student body provides a truly unique opportunity.

After touring the campus, I believe the community atmosphere and small classes will be a great learning environment. As a result of talking with you and because of how "at home" I felt on campus, I am confident that the School of International Studies is a good fit and have decided to apply for early decision.

Thank you again for your assistance in the application process. I am excited about the next steps.

Signature
Name
Phone
Email address
LinkedIn address

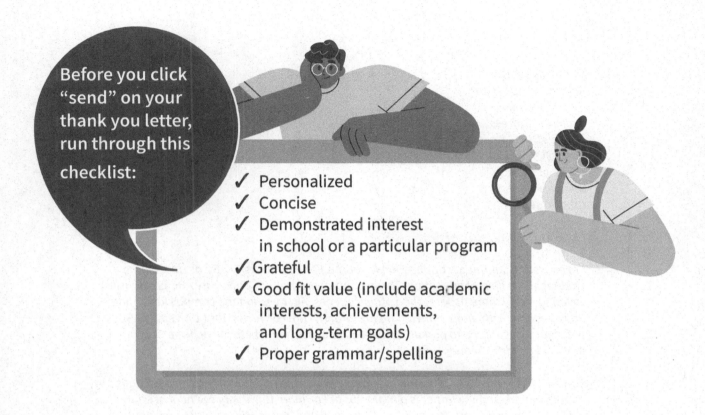

Before you click "send" on your thank you letter, run through this checklist:

- ✓ Personalized
- ✓ Concise
- ✓ Demonstrated interest in school or a particular program
- ✓ Grateful
- ✓ Good fit value (include academic interests, achievements, and long-term goals)
- ✓ Proper grammar/spelling

Sample cover letter: A college application cover letter/email accompanies your admissions packet or Common App and is the first document a college admission committee will see. This is your chance to impress the admission officer and stand out. You must demonstrate that you have something unique to offer and why you will be a great addition to the campus. The letter also provides an opportunity for applicants to explain a special circumstance, like a GPA drop due to parental illness.

The letter should include the college-bound student's interests, goals, and motivations and why the applicant would be a good fit for the college. Make sure to check the requirements of each college before writing the letter and comply with them. Refer to the example on the next page:

Name of Applicant
Address of Applicant
City, State, Zip
LinkedIn address
Today's Date
Admission Officer's Name
Name of College
College Address
City, State, Zip

Dear Ms./Mr. XYZ,

I'm excited to submit my application for admission to University ABC as an aspiring student in the field of education. The education program at University ABC is extensive, covering many more aspects than other colleges. After visiting the campus last month and speaking with alumni (including my father), I am convinced that University ABC is the ideal place for me to pursue my college education and help me achieve my goal of teaching children in middle school.

Education is in my DNA. I grew up in a family of educators. My mother teaches English in middle school, and my father is a professor at Fordham University's School of Education. My father is a proud graduate of ABC University and frequently shares stories about campus life and the professors he most admired. I have always found the field of education fascinating and rewarding, and direct experience has reinforced my desire to major in it. Throughout high school, I have been volunteering as a tutor at the local Boys & Girls Club during Homework Hour. In fact, I created a virtual tutoring service in April 2020 to help middle school children with homework and boost their skills during the pandemic. My ultimate goal is to get my PhD in Education.

My parental influence, academic background, and accomplishments have prepared me for success. I am a highly motivated student with good academic, athletic, and interpersonal skills. I understand that qualities such as enthusiasm, resilience, diligence, focus, and commitment are needed in the education field. I will be graduating this spring with a 3.9 GPA and take great pride in the many honors I have achieved. I started a local chapter of the National Society of High School Scholars (NSHSS) last year at my high school and currently serve as president. It has grown to be one of the largest chapters on the East Coast with 38 members. I am also an active member of the English Literary Club and participate on the lacrosse team. These endeavors make me a great fit for University ABC. I'm confident that I will be an asset to the educational field and University ABC, both as a student and alumnus.

All of the required documentation is enclosed with this letter. I appreciate your time and consideration and look forward to the next steps.

Sincerely,

Applicant signature
Printed name of Applicant
LinkedIn Address
Enclosure: Application form, SAT scores, résumé, essay, recommendation letters

Before you click "send" on your cover letter, run through this checklist of essential items that warrant inclusion:

✓ Legacy: Do you have any family who graduated from the school?
✓ Academic interests
✓ Demonstrated interest in school or particular program
✓ Required attachments/documentation
✓ Good fit value (include academic interests, achievements, and long-term goals)
✓ Proper grammar/spelling

Sample letter of continued interest (LOCI): Getting waitlisted or deferred from a dream school is disappointing. The good news is that you can and should take action by writing a letter of continued interest (LOCI). A LOCI lets the college know that the applicant has a strong desire to attend the school and demonstrates why the admissions office should still consider the application. The one-page letter should be completed within a couple of weeks of receiving your deferral notification.

The letter updates the college on any new achievements or activities since your original application and hopefully convinces them that you will be a positive contributor to the freshman class. The keyword here is *new*. Don't bother presenting accomplishments or information already shared in your original application. Instead, provide information that strengthens your application, such as updates on extracurricular activities, improved GPA or standardized test scores, and your continued interest in attending the school. Perhaps you can share your experience during a recent visit to the campus and reinforce your love of the school.

Lastly, follow the directions the college provides for the next steps. Should you be deferred, follow the guidelines laid out by the college. If they specifically ask you not to send a letter, don't!

Refer to the example on the following page of a LOCI that checks all the boxes:

Name of Applicant
Address of Applicant
City, State, Zip
Today's Date
Admission Officer's Name
Name of College
College Address
City, State, Zip

Dear Ms./Mr. XYZ,

Thank you for taking the time to review my application and offering me an opportunity to be on the waitlist. I'm writing to express my continued interest in majoring in computer engineering as part of the ABC University School of Engineering and to update the admissions committee on some recent accomplishments and activities.

Since applying in January, I received a Microsoft Technology Associate (MTA) Database Certification, which has given me a strong foundation in database theory and design. I am applying this learning to a spring internship at the National Aeronautics and Space Administration (NASA). I have had the opportunity to work with exceptional mentors on database management, cloud applications, and relational database design. I also won an ISEF award in the Systems Software category. My goal is to equip myself with a strong base of knowledge to get me off to a running start in college. This honor means a lot to me and demonstrates my passion and commitment to computer engineering.

ABC's University School of Engineering—with ten different majors and fifteen minors—has the most innovative and broadest engineering curricula in the US. As a motivated problem-solver and creative thinker, I can contribute positively to academic and campus life.

I remain optimistic and dedicated to attending ABC University if accepted and appreciate your time and consideration. Please let me know if you have any questions relating to the additional information.

Sincerely,

Applicant signature
Printed name of Applicant
Enclosure: Application form, SAT scores, résumé, essay, recommendation letters

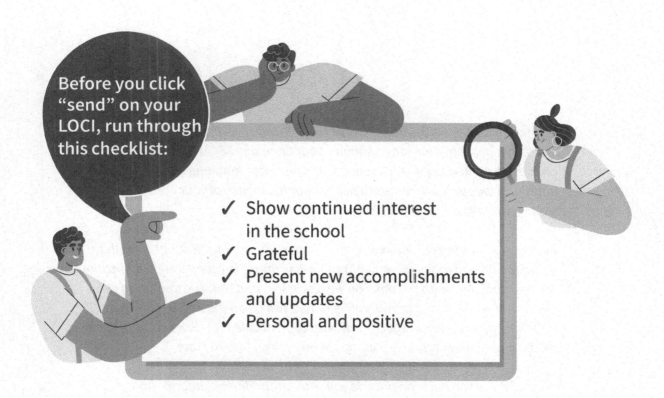

Before you click "send" on your LOCI, run through this checklist:

✓ Show continued interest in the school
✓ Grateful
✓ Present new accomplishments and updates
✓ Personal and positive

Sample thank you letter for a job or internship interview: Make sure to send an email or thank you note promptly (within 24 hours) after the interview. Similar to the college thank you letter, the note should be brief (two to three paragraphs) and express gratitude for the interviewer's time. Reinforce your interest in the organization/position and why you would be a great fit. Personalization is key — include a topic of mutual interest that came up during your interview. Refer to the example on the next page of a sample thank you note:

Dear Ms./Mrs. XYZ:

Thank you for taking the time to meet with me today to discuss the social media internship position. Our conversation about Company ABC's expansion made me even more excited to join the team and support your marketing goals. In addition, I was very impressed to hear about the launch of your upcoming summit in Davos.

As discussed during our interview, I am extremely passionate about everything social media and intend to major in communications in college. My qualifications are well-matched with the position we discussed, and I believe my strong work ethic, writing skills, and collaborative nature will be an asset to the company. In addition, my experience, specifically with content calendar development, social media management, and reporting are very relevant to the role.

Please let me know if I can provide you with any additional information or references. I appreciate your consideration for this role and am confident that I'd be a great addition to the team. I look forward to hearing from you regarding next steps.

Sincerely,

Signature
Name
Phone
Email address

Before you click "send" on your thank you letter, run through this checklist:

✓ Concise
✓ Enthusiastic
✓ Personalized
✓ Grateful
✓ Demonstrate interest in position and/or company
✓ Good fit value
✓ Proper grammar/spelling

Email etiquette

Texting no doubt comes second nature to you. But since many teens may not have extensive experience with email, let's end this section with a look at some email etiquette best practices:

- Emailing a thank you note is common and perfectly acceptable.
- Have a clear and simple subject line.
- Choose between formal or first name basis, based on company culture/interview outcome.
- Interviews with more than one person: Send personalized notes to each participant or a collective note to the group. You can also write a single note to your primary interviewer and reference the other participants.

Writing the right way

To wrap up this section, I want to stress the importance of communication skills. In this era of keyboards and smartphones, you may think that writing skills don't matter as much as they used to. After all, it's all about IRLs and LOLs these days, so who cares about grammar?

However, take note. An investment in writing is an investment in yourself! Believe it or not, great writing can make a big difference in your career. Writing is a skill anyone can improve with practice. You may want to consider taking a writing class. Even if you never write a paper again after high school, learning how to articulate your thoughts can enhance your communication skills as well as your self-confidence and leadership abilities.

When it comes to communication, writing and speaking go hand-in-hand. Writing can help you hone your presentation skills and help you communicate your ideas more effectively — whether it's in an email, essay, interview, or live presentation.

BRANDAMENTALS

Here are some top takeaways to keep top of mind:

1 **Know what makes a key message work.** Before you put pen to paper, make sure you fully understand what makes a powerful key message. Every key message should be concise, relevant, memorable, compelling, and positive.

2 **Make your key messages interlock.**
Key messages should complement each other and all point toward a single, overarching theme: Your Uniquely Me statement.

3 **Use your key messages often.** Once your key messages are crafted, deploy them liberally. They should be woven into your college applications, cover letters, emails, and in-person interviews.

4 **Be persistent and polite.** Your audience needs to hear your key messages more than once for them to stick. If you surfaced them in an email correspondence, bring them up again in an in-person interview. If waitlisted, use the key messages to present new achievements in a Letter of Continued Intent (LOCI).

5 **Stay on brand.**
Maintain a consistent voice across different channels. Ensure your LinkedIn, Facebook, Twitter, and other profiles are up-to-date and in harmony.

PART IV – YOUR PERSONAL BRANDING TOOLKIT

Assembling an Impressive Online Portfolio

This section builds upon the previous Messaging section and helps you craft a **captivating online portfolio**. An online portfolio consists of various items to "market" yourself to admission officers, recruiters, and your network. These items may include your online profiles, website, blog, résumé, and cover letter. Every representation of you reinforces your brand, so remain professional and consistent across the board.

Your social media accounts are a key part of the college application process and require as much scrutiny as the college essay — perhaps even more. The type of person you describe in your college application needs to be in sync with your social media accounts. The same thing applies to job interviews. Indeed, it has become commonplace for admission officers and job recruiters to conduct screening of applicants' online profiles. And so, your accounts should help answer questions like: Why should a highly selective college choose you? Why should you get a merit aid award? Why should you be hired over other applicants?

So, how do you make an online portfolio that's polished and professional? Get started with a cleanup, removing dormant, off-brand, and inappropriate profiles.

Cleanup Tips

1 **Audit your online presence.** Start with a Google search. What appears when you Google your name? Review the results and ensure there are no inappropriate images or content. Anything controversial, discriminatory, or downright mean should be removed from social platforms. This includes images containing nudity, alcohol, drugs, or offensive language. If someone has posted a questionable photo, you should ask them to remove it or untag you. Also, edit existing posts for typos and grammatical errors and delete negative or controversial comments on your posts.

2 **Choose appropriate usernames and handles.** A professional email address is a must for college-bound students. An email address will be part of your identity for a long time, so avoid cutesy or inappropriate nicknames (e.g., kissmybutt@gmail.com, hothannah@gmail.com). Instead, create a new email address that is recognizable and professional (e.g., firstnamelastname@gmail.com). Don't worry: emails from an old account can easily be forwarded to a newly created one.

An important note: It's not a good idea to delete your profile because it doesn't guarantee the data is completely gone. Plus, it looks like you're trying to hide something.

Ultimately, you should come across as a responsible young person who would be a welcome member of a college campus. If your posts contradict this goal, remove them. Looking like a partier online may seem "cool" to your friends, but it doesn't impress college admissions officers. And take heed: rather than solely focusing on the "clean up," also emphasize building out your social media presence for college. We'll discuss this further in the *Managing Your Social Media* Presence chapter.

The Truth about Privacy and Texting

When applying for college, some teens resort to shutting down their social media accounts entirely or trying to hide their online identities.

Maximizing privacy settings gives you (and your parents) a sense of security to post more freely. But maximizing privacy settings is not foolproof — a private post can still become public. Plus, should you decide to follow college social media accounts of interest, your account will no longer be private to the college.

Many students choose to create alternative accounts, which is the best option. Why? Personal and college-oriented social media activities do not mix. The content you should be sharing with colleges is far different than the content you communicate with friends and peers. Different audiences demand different content — that's the first rule of marketing.

And if you think your text messages are different from your social media profiles, think again. There's no such thing as privacy when it comes to your phone. You share your deepest secrets and thoughts and hit "send", confident that they'll remain between you and the recipient. And for the most part, that's true — but things can and do go wrong.

Text messages can be screenshot and shared without your knowledge or permission, leaving you with no control over who sees them or where they land. Screenshots of racist and inflammatory text conversations have gone viral countless times. So before you hit "send" on that next text message, ask yourself: Would I be comfortable with that message scrolling across the Times Square digital billboard?

YOUR TOOLKIT

Instagram	**YouTube**
Twitter/Facebook	**Build a website with a blog, an "about me"**
Blogging or Podcasting	**section, certifications, and contact page**

Best Platforms to Invest in

With the cleanup complete, it's time to create a digital presence that differentiates you and tells your story — your talents, passions, achievements, and more. It's here that you may feel overwhelmed by the vast array of social media platforms. Start to narrow down the list by determining which ones are the best match for you. Are you an artist? Then Pinterest and Instagram work best. Are you seeking a career in broadcasting? Then stick to YouTube or TikTok. Below are a handful of the most commonly used channels:

LinkedIn

Overview: LinkedIn is the most beneficial channel to showcase your achievements during the college application process. The ideal age to establish a LinkedIn presence is age 16. The platform allows you to connect with college admissions officers, college professors, department heads, and alumni. Getting a jump start on LinkedIn will let you take charge of your narrative in a professional manner and set the stage for your career path. Since admissions officers favor well-rounded applicants, it is best to show a mix of academics, leadership, and community service on your profile.

Who should leverage: Everyone. All students should have a LinkedIn profile.

Note: LinkedIn is such an important tool that we devoted a whole chapter to it.

Instagram

Overview: Instagram is an online photo- and video-sharing app. It is one of the most widely used social media platforms by teenagers, with more than one billion active users. Facebook acquired Instagram in 2012.

Who should leverage: Students oriented toward the visual arts, photography, and theater, since the platform is ideal for showcasing artwork of all stripes. Instagram is also an excellent tool for athletes to share their team spirit and athletic prowess. Pinterest and Flickr are similar platforms to consider for those with a visual portfolio.

YouTube

Overview: The most popular video-sharing website globally, YouTube is synonymous with the internet for many people. It's home to content by countless creators and businesses.

Who should leverage: Athletes, theater students, and anyone who believes that video would be compelling to share their story. For example, long- and short-term videos of you scoring the winning goal or making that amazing play are sure to catch admissions officers' attention. A similar platform for uploading videos is Vimeo, which is currently ad-free and has a more professional feel.

ZeeMee

Overview: This social media platform helps college applicants add color to their applications in the form of photos, videos, and text. You can also view the profile of other prospective students and chat with them. Some students even find their college roommates through ZeeMee. The platform allows you to add an introductory video, answer pre-set questions, and upload original content.

Who should leverage: If you're applying to one of the colleges that use ZeeMee, then definitely add a link to your profile on the Common App or Coalition App. Schools such as WashU St. Louis, Carnegie Mellon, and Bucknell have adapted ZeeMee as part of their optional application components.

(You're probably wondering: What about Facebook? Although Facebook is the largest social network, few teens use the platform these days, so we decided not to include it in this list. But you can still use Facebook to build a college-centric profile or engage with colleges of interest.)

EXERCISE: What Does Social Media Mean to You?

It is important to take an inventory of your own social media life. Time for some self-reflection: Is social media currently having a positive or negative effect on your life?

_____

_____

_____

Do you believe that social media "likes" and "favorites" are a reflection of popularity? If so, what are some of the types of things that you are most "popular" for sharing?

_____

_____

_____

Sharing photos/videos can be a powerful and memorable way to communicate and present information. What examples of photos/videos might someone share that can be <u>positive</u> and <u>helpful</u> to their brand?

_____

_____

_____

Lots of people follow and are followed by strangers. How might this actually be a good thing in building a brand?

_____

_____

_____

What specific ways can YOU use social media to share "the best" things about yourself?

_____

_____

_____

Think about the last five posts you made on your favorite social network. Would your college of choice or job recruiter be impressed by any or all of them?

_____

_____

_____

Do you allow/would you let your parents follow ALL of your social accounts? Explain.

_____

_____

_____

What is the most positive experience you have had related to social media?

_____

_____

_____

In Anderson Cooper's documentary, *#Being 13*, one of the teens stated that "everyone talks about everyone on social media." If this is true, what would you hope people are saying about you?

_____

_____

_____

In your opinion, is it okay to act entirely differently online than you do in the "real" world? What are the implications of that?

_____

_____

_____

Creating an Unforgettable Profile

Once you've selected which platforms to invest in, it's time to start building. To get you on your way, here are four tips for creating an unforgettable profile:

> The *"ultimate secret"* to winning admissions and earning scholarships is to distinguish yourself from others in a meaningful way. You have to be seen as one in ten. If you do, say, or write what everyone else does, then you are in the pack of nine... indistinguishable!
>
> – Hans Hanson, Founder and CEO, College Logic, Connecticut

1 **Create a custom LinkedIn URL.** URLs can be ugly, a never-ending string of letters and numbers. But they don't have to be. On LinkedIn, you can create a customized URL, like http://www.linkedin.com/in/yourname. If your name has already been snatched up, select a variation — perhaps use a middle name or initial. A customized URL will allow others to find and connect with you easily. You can also match your custom LinkedIn URL with your social media handles.

2 **Put your best face forward.** It's time to say farewell to childish and inappropriate profile photos. Put away those Snapchat stickers and cartoon avatars and focus on making a good impression. Use a headshot from the shoulder level up with professional attire and a neutral background. And use the same photo across all social media platforms for consistency. Lastly, high-resolution photos (minimum 300 DPI) are a must.

3 **Write an epic bio.** A good bio needs to be concise yet communicate a lot: interests, strengths, and talents. Think of it as a 30-second elevator pitch that sums up who you are and what value you bring. Include awards, media coverage, and, if you're feeling creative, your all-time favorite quote. Once completed, don't forget to add your bio to all your social accounts.

4 **Showcase your academics, achievements, and activities.** Make sure to highlight a diverse range of interests: academic pursuits, creative endeavors, hobbies, and volunteer work. You need to build a portfolio that displays a passion for your intended course of study, be it engineering, nutrition, social work, fashion, or something else entirely. At the same time, make sure that positive character attributes surface, too, like leadership, resiliency, teamwork, and volunteer service. As mentioned in the "Finding the Perfect Adjectives that Describe you" activity, these are traits that college admission officers and job recruiters value.

Stand Up and Stand Out

Before heading to the next section, here are three more steps you can take to stand out in the application process:

■ **Build a personal website.** While this may seem a time-consuming task, it is well worth the effort. Having a personal website is a great way to showcase your talents, achievements, extracurricular activities, volunteerism, and portfolio of work. And it can serve as a hub for the other channels you are engaged with. It's relatively easy to choose a website platform (e.g., Squarespace, WordPress), register a domain, and select a web hosting plan. The more difficult task is your domain name. And just as important as building an attractive and content-rich website is maintaining it. Don't let it stay dormant; constantly refresh with new content and updates on your achievements.

■ **Maximize your email signature line.** This is great real estate — don't waste it. Include your full name, grade/high school name, address, and cell phone number. You may also want to include a good-quality photo, website hyperlink (if applicable), and hyperlinked social media icons. Also consider including a unique honor, like valedictorian.

■ **Create a video.** According to Forrester Research, one minute of video is worth 1.8 million words. So you may want to share your narrative through video and embed a link in your correspondence. If you decide to make such a video, be sure to stay on message, speak clearly (rehearsing helps), dress conservatively, choose an appropriate background (not your bedroom), and do a few takes of the video before selecting the one you like best. Also, keep it brief: 90 seconds or less.

BRANDAMENTALS

Here are some takeaways to keep in mind
as you build your online presence:

1 **Audit your online presence.** Before you begin the college admissions process, search your name online and take note to see how you show up. Developing a strong online profile and digital footprint is essential.

2 **Shore up your accounts.** Make sure your social media accounts are reputable — no party photos or inappropriate comment threads. Assume college admissions counselors can and will read each post.

3 **Invest in the right platforms.** Think beyond which social media platforms are hip. Instead, think about which ones best accentuate your strengths. For example: If you're an artist, it may be wise to open an Instagram account for your artwork.

4 **Consider all your touch points.** Personal branding is more than just an online profile — it's a holistic picture that can make or break college admissions and career opportunities. Consider every communication mode, including e-mail, cell phones, interviews, etc.

PART V — BUILDING YOUR DIGITAL PORTFOLIO ON LINKEDIN

LinkedIn Is All That

If you're thinking about elite colleges, you probably know that students who get turned down are often just as strong as those that are accepted. That's why you need to use tools that make you stand out to admissions officers and others who could help elevate your application, such as professors or interviewers. So use social media to your benefit, showcasing your interests, character, community service, and other strengths.

To make a great impression, get familiar with LinkedIn. LinkedIn may not be as glamorous as other platforms, but what it lacks in glitz, it more than makes up for in usefulness. Almost all colleges have a LinkedIn presence, and they encourage engagement with faculty, students, alumni, and administrators. From recruitment to networking, LinkedIn has become *the* go-to resource for colleges and employers.

LinkedIn allows teens 16 and over to set up an account, yet only 9 percent of high school students use the platform (Pew Research, 2018). This is a big opportunity for you. Step up your college application game now and join LinkedIn!

You may be thinking: *Most high school students don't have professional work experience.* Or *LinkedIn is a platform for job seekers and businesses.* But in reality, LinkedIn is a priceless resource for academic and career success. It gives insight into who you are as a person: your talents, your interests, and your accomplishments. Students can showcase their volunteer work, community service, organizations, and hobbies, even if these activities are not related to their specific field of study. You can showcase real examples of your writing, photography, or other talents directly on your profile.

What sets LinkedIn apart from other major social media platforms is that it's not built on existing friendships. LinkedIn provides a means to network with people you may not currently know but share common interests with — like a certain college or area of study.

Understanding Your LinkedIn Network Reach

On LinkedIn, people in your network are called "Connections." Your LinkedIn network is made up of your first-degree, second-degree, and third-degree connections and also fellow members of your LinkedIn groups. People outside this network may not be able to discover your profile.

Social Assurity

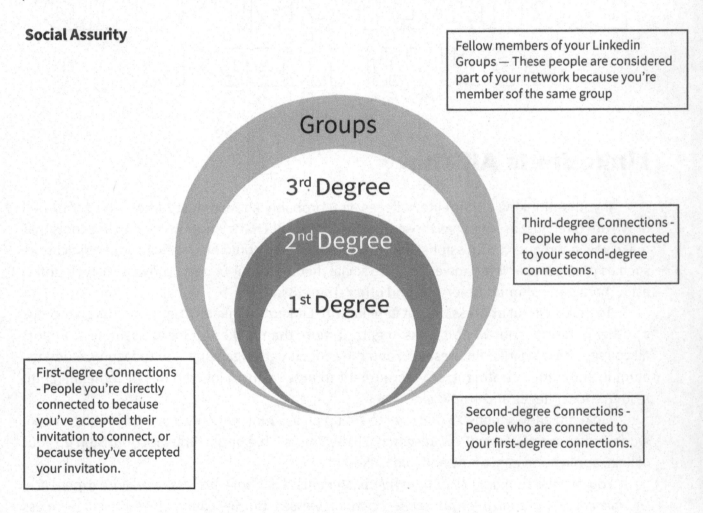

Fellow members of your Linkedin Groups — These people are considered part of your network because you're member sof the same group

Third-degree Connections - People who are connected to your second-degree connections.

First-degree Connections - People you're directly connected to because you've accepted their invitation to connect, or because they've accepted your invitation.

Second-degree Connections - People who are connected to your first-degree connections.

First-degree Connections - People you're directly connected to because you've accepted their invitation to connect, or because they've accepted your invitation. You'll see a first-degree icon next to their name in search results and on their profile. Once connected, you can contact them directly by sending a message.

Second-degree Connections - People who are connected to your first-degree connections. You'll see a second-degree icon next to their name in search results and on their profile. You can send them an invitation by clicking "Connect."

Third-degree Connections - People who are connected to your second-degree connections. You'll see a third-degree icon next to their name in search results and on their profile.

As a student, chances are you don't currently have many people to connect with. But perhaps you have a close relationship with a teacher, counselor, coach, family member, or friend who will be your mentor. This is a great start, and LinkedIn gives you the opportunity to grow this network.

Stellar LinkedIn Profile Samples

Mirei Dominguez
Playwright I Performing Artist I Singer I Production I Drama
Student at Fiorello H. La Guardia High School, Class of 2020
New York City Metropolitan Area • 15 Connections

createHER

Fiorello H. La Guardia High School

I am an aspiring playwright and actor. For as long as I can remember, I've had a deep connection with the arts and different forms of human expression. Starting as a little girl with my obsession for movie musicals (thanks mom!), I pursued singing, performing, and later, storytelling. I fell in love with the imaginary worlds I could create, the limitless possibilities with just a pen, paper and an idea. Through my work, I hope to explore the complexities of human relationships, what it means to be a person in a workd that is increasingly divisive, and other essential truths about the way we live.

Along the way, I want to make art that can form a more healthy society; one that is inclusive of everybody's stories and experiences despite race, gender, body type, socioeconomic status, and other marginalized identities. One of my missions in theater and, hopefully, my career, is to promote a Broadway that looks as diverse as our world. This means including stories for and about people of color, those who are differently abled, and other communities that are so often silenced.

On a personal note, I am an avid reader and I appreciate all forms of music. Ultimately, I am someone who loves to laugh, be around people I care about, and experience things.

Featured

Most colleges have moved away from looking at résumés. They were too long, inconsistent, and impossible to compare. That's not the case with LinkedIn.

The area containing your profile photo, name, and descriptive headline is what colleges and recruiters will see first, and it's the most important real estate on your LinkedIn profile. At a minimum, a strong LinkedIn profile picture includes a pleasant smile and professional attire. LinkedIn's search algorithm places a priority on displaying profiles with images in search results. Without a picture, your profile won't get the full consideration or visibility it deserves.

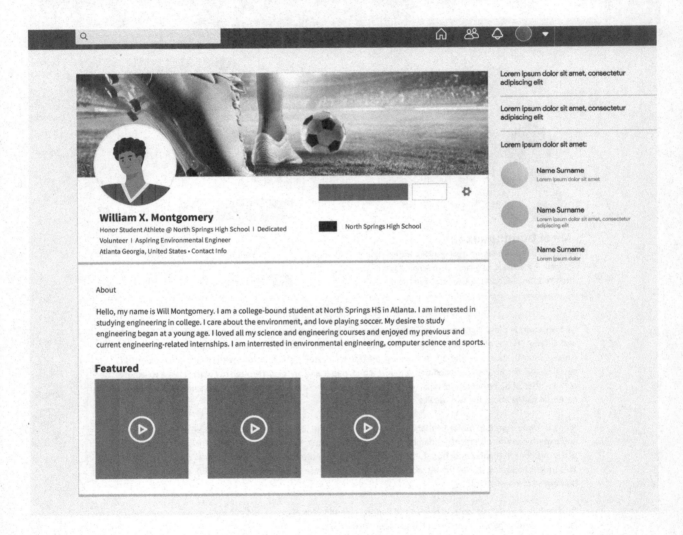

Just like a newspaper headline, your LinkedIn headline is meant to stimulate enough interest to make the reader want to learn more about you. Your LinkedIn headline should also be written with SEO in mind.

Your LinkedIn summary allows you to showcase your authentic self. You can be more personal than on your résumé, personal statement, or college application. The summary is a chance to make an unforgettable first impression on college admissions officers and other key people.

Although LinkedIn allows up to 2,600 characters for the summary, there's no need to use them all. For high school students, the LinkedIn summary should capture the same skills and personal attributes you plan to highlight in your college essay.

After you add your summary to LinkedIn, bring the text to life with multimedia. LinkedIn allows you to add videos, pictures, links, and documents to your profile, reinforcing your words.

When building your LinkedIn profile, don't underestimate your non-school experiences. Colleges are more impressed with a student who earns money for their family or who cares for their siblings than they are with a student who enrolls in an expensive summer program. Talk about projects you've worked on and the problems you've solved, and add organizations you belong to.

In the days of résumés, people added references at the bottom of their documents. But there wasn't room for those people to elaborate on their accomplishments, so these references were easy to overlook. But not so with LinkedIn. You can invite people who know you and your work, like teachers and coaches, to write glowing, in-depth recommendations. And whoever views your profile can read them.

By creating a LinkedIn profile, you're also making yourself more visible across the whole web: LinkedIn taps into the indexing power of Google.

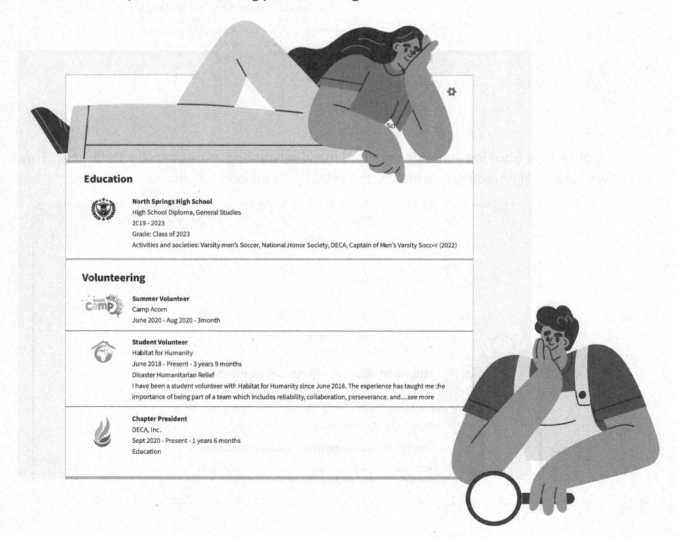

Education

North Springs High School
High School Diploma, General Studies
2019 - 2023
Grade: Class of 2023
Activities and societies: Varsity men's Soccer, National Honor Society, DECA, Captain of Men's Varsity Soccer (2022)

Volunteering

Summer Volunteer
Camp Acorn
June 2020 - Aug 2020 - 3month

Student Volunteer
Habitat for Humanity
June 2018 - Present - 3 years 9 months
Disaster Humanitarian Relief
I have been a student volunteer with Habitat for Humanity since June 2018. The experience has taught me the importance of being part of a team which includes reliability, collaboration, perseverance, and....see more

Chapter President
DECA, Inc.
Sept 2020 - Present - 1 years 6 months
Education

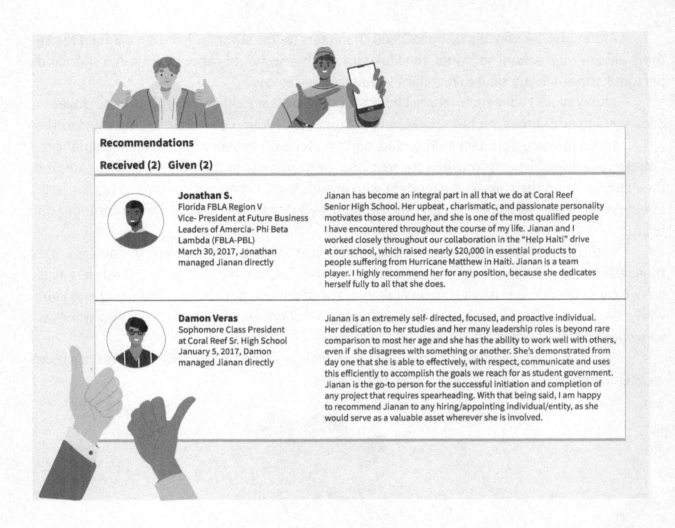

Recommendations

Received (2) Given (2)

Jonathan S.
Florida FBLA Region V
Vice- President at Future Business
Leaders of Amercia- Phi Beta
Lambda (FBLA-PBL)
March 30, 2017, Jonathan
managed Jianan directly

Jianan has become an integral part in all that we do at Coral Reef Senior High School. Her upbeat , charismatic, and passionate personality motivates those around her, and she is one of the most qualified people I have encountered throughout the course of my life. Jianan and I worked closely throughout our collaboration in the "Help Haiti" drive at our school, which raised nearly $20,000 in essential products to people suffering from Hurricane Matthew in Haiti. Jianan is a team player. I highly recommend her for any position, because she dedicates herself fully to all that she does.

Damon Veras
Sophomore Class President
at Coral Reef Sr. High School
January 5, 2017, Damon
managed Jianan directly

Jianan is an extremely self- directed, focused, and proactive individual. Her dedication to her studies and her many leadership roles is beyond rare comparison to most her age and she has the ability to work well with others, even if she disagrees with something or another. She's demonstrated from day one that she is able to effectively, with respect, communicate and uses this efficiently to accomplish the goals we reach for as student government. Jianan is the go-to person for the successful initiation and completion of any project that requires spearheading. With that being said, I am happy to recommend Jianan to any hiring/appointing individual/entity, as she would serve as a valuable asset wherever she is involved.

Notice how Google even indexes your LinkedIn headline and summary statement. This is a powerful digital branding tool for you to control your digital footprint.

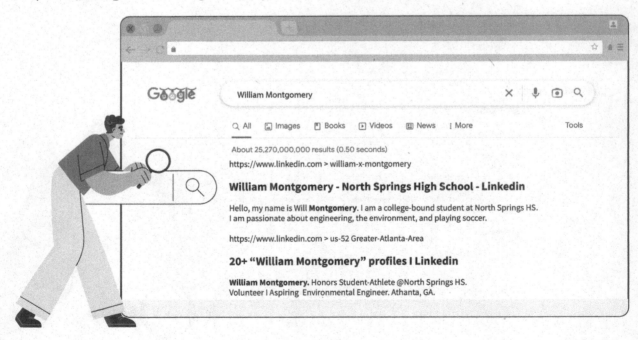

Still, simply having a LinkedIn profile does not guarantee that people will find you. You need to draw people's attention by engaging and "putting yourself out there." The good news is that there's a chapter on Networking to help you master this critical skill. Networking may not come easy at first. But with practice, you'll see how quickly you can master it. You'll also be surprised by how much people admire teens with goals and ambitions!

On LinkedIn, connections are relationships of trust between people. If you're connected to someone, you will see each other's shares and updates on your respective home pages. You can also easily send messages to your connections on LinkedIn.

Following someone on LinkedIn allows you to see the person's posts and articles on your homepage without being connected to them. However, the person you are following won't see your posts. You can reach a larger audience by allowing others to follow your activity and read what you're sharing on LinkedIn.

You can also follow colleges and businesses on LinkedIn. Here's how:

Step 1 - Register on the college website before following the college on LinkedIn (or any other social media platform). A "Request Information" or "Learn More" tab can typically be found on the admissions page of the college website. Sometimes the tab is buried, so you may need to search for it.

Step 2 - Complete the online form in its entirety, making sure that the email you provide is the same email you used to validate your LinkedIn profile and the same one you will be using when applying to college. You will then receive a confirmation email. Open it!

Follow a college's feed to stay current on events happening at the college. Engage in conversations that are meaningful to you. Remember that there are people managing this feed who will potentially be looking at your profile.

BRANDAMENTALS

Here are some takeaways to deliver the best you have to offer:

1 **LinkedIn is an essential tool — use it.** The popular platform isn't just for professionals. It's also for ambitious teens who want to stand out.

2 **LinkedIn is perfect for showcasing your brand.** You can curate your image to a tee by leveraging a unique URL, professional headshot, compelling summary section, and more.

3 **LinkedIn can kick-start networking.** LinkedIn allows you to build a rich network without leaving your desk. You can connect and correspond with college admissions officers, professionals in your intended field, and like-minded students.

SECTION C: DELIVERY

PART VI – MANAGING YOUR SOCIAL MEDIA PRESENCE

Your messages are honed, and your new and improved social media profiles are activated. Now what? This section will help you use these in a meaningful and deliberate way. While many headlines these days focus on the negative impacts of social media, there are also decidedly positive effects. While excellent grades and academic rigor will continue to be the primary metric for college admissions, your chances for acceptance will greatly improve once you learn to leverage social media to showcase skills, personal attributes, demonstrated interest, and good character.

Every day, social media becomes more and more ingrained in our lives. So it's no surprise that colleges are turning to social media to find the best and the brightest students.

Using Social Media to Your Advantage

The Oxford dictionary defines "digital footprint" as the information about a particular person that exists on the internet as a result of their online activity. Your digital footprint fuels your online reputation. And by the time high school rolls around, most teens have amassed a sizable chunk of reviewable online activity.

Back in 2008, the idea that colleges or employers would pass judgment about you by viewing your social media was a controversial topic. Social media was still very much a novelty, and the social media platform of the day, Facebook, was generally dismissed as a passing teenage infatuation. In those early days, social media was seen as a playground where teens behaved impulsively and spontaneously without fear of consequence. Postings were intentionally outrageous and left a trail of shallow, reactive, unimpressive, and immature content.

Colleges and employers now openly rely on these digital footprints to make important assessments about applicants. Assessments like who they are, what they value, and how they treat others. Kaplan Test Prep first began tracking this practice in 2008, when only 10 percent of college admissions officers from the most selective colleges reported viewing applicants' social media profiles. Predictably, the digital footprints seen by colleges in the early days of social media did not bode well for students. Thus, the myth was born that a discoverable social media presence can only damage your chances of finding a job or gaining acceptance into college.

"Schools can now get a complete picture of their applicants, including what they're saying and thinking about them on Facebook, LinkedIn, Instagram, and Twitter — which could be even more meaningful than traditional data points like GPA and SAT."

— THE CHRONICLE OF HIGHER EDUCATION

10 Must-Know Tips to Leverage Social Media for College Admissions

Tip #1: Know the four tenets of social media.

You are never anonymous. Your posts will never disappear. Anyone can find everything you've ever posted. And people are listening. These four rules apply to all social media platforms, including Snapchat, TikTok, and Instagram/Finsta.

The social media landscape has shifted enormously over the years and will undoubtedly continue to evolve. 15 years ago, just about all teenage social media activity was happening on Facebook. Initially, social media reviews by colleges were relatively simple. Since Facebook indexes every post, comment, mention, tag, like, share, and follow, it was extremely easy to find and assess anyone's digital trail. All a college admissions officer needed to do was open Facebook and perform a basic search. And so they did.

Around 2012, students became aware that colleges and employers were using Facebook to "stalk" their applicants. As a result, people feared that students might be losing out on college admissions, scholarship money, and job opportunities because of their online presence. In response, some "experts" advised teens to delete their social media accounts, while other "experts" advised teens to go on a complete social media lockdown. Neither worked.

Social media had become the central hub of teen social life, so neither deleting nor barricading social media was ever a realistic option. Instead, most teens simply placed an alias on their Facebook profile while migrating edgier and more self-reflective social media content away from Facebook and onto newer, youth-oriented platforms like Tumblr and Instagram. By 2016, teen flight from Facebook peaked as both Instagram and the newly hot app Snapchat (which falsely promised the gift of impermanence) experienced significant teen growth. These platforms overtook Facebook as the most popular social media app for teens and, together with TikTok, remain popular to this day.

As teens moved their unfiltered social media activity off Facebook and began curating their feeds elsewhere, colleges began realizing that the low-hanging fruit of easily discoverable and objectionable social media content was gone. But despite these changes, many colleges were still willing to look at social media. Why? Gaining acceptance to the best colleges was becoming more and more competitive. College admissions officers realized they could still use social media to learn about their applicants and perhaps find tangible reasons to take one applicant over another.

So does hiding social media really give you any competitive advantage under this framework?

No! With almost all high school and college students active on social media, not being found when someone is looking can be

Know the 4 Tenets of Social Media

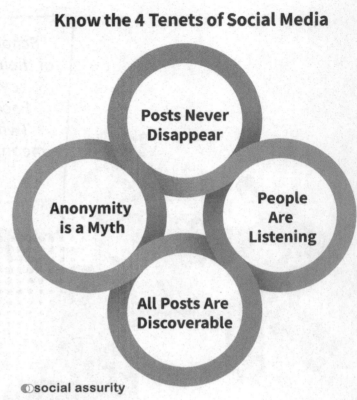

Ⓓsocial assurity

fatal for most applicants. So unless your social media is hurtful, hateful, violent, illegal, or pornographic, students really have nothing to hide. Being playful, having some fun while growing up, and showing some imperfections at an early age is nothing to worry about. It's perfectly normal and acceptable conduct.

What is important is ensuring your key social media profiles and content are robust, uniquely easy to find, and aligned with your college and employment aspirations.

Tip #2: "Nothing to hide" is not the same as "something to show."

"I know colleges might be looking at my social media, so I've never posted anything that can embarrass me." We hear this from students all the time and ask whether they're certain about this (see Tip #1). Then we remind them that the lack of a digital presence will not help their college admissions chances. If colleges are looking, you might as well give them something to see.

Let's fast-forward to 2022, where social media continues to play an integral role in teen culture — and where TikTok, Instagram, Snapchat, Twitter, Pinterest, YouTube, and LinkedIn have all joined (and even surpassed) Facebook on the main digital stage. Recent surveys indicate that over 95 percent of American teens are actively using social media, and these teens are online almost nine hours a day, not including time for homework. The pandemic only seems to have accelerated this trend: 63 percent of parents report seeing their teen's social media use increase since the start of the COVID-19 pandemic. Also, social media is no longer strictly child's play, as over 70 percent of American adults are active on at least one social media platform.

Kaplan Test Prep's most recent social media survey found that 66 percent of college admissions officers believe that incorporating applicants' social media pages into their acceptance decisions is "fair game." If two-thirds of college reviewers are open to looking at social media, then any applicant hiding or who has not been curating their social media profiles for college has missed a golden opportunity. Social media can be used to build a digital presence that advances your academic and career objectives in unique and powerful ways. When it comes to college admissions and employment pursuits, students will be assessed on factors beyond their grades, test scores, and résumés. Soft skills, character attributes, and core values can often be culled from social media feeds.

Tip #3: Create specific content for your intended audiences.

Personal and college-oriented social media activities do not mix. The content students should share with colleges is very different from the content they should share with their friends and peers. Different audiences demand different content and channels.

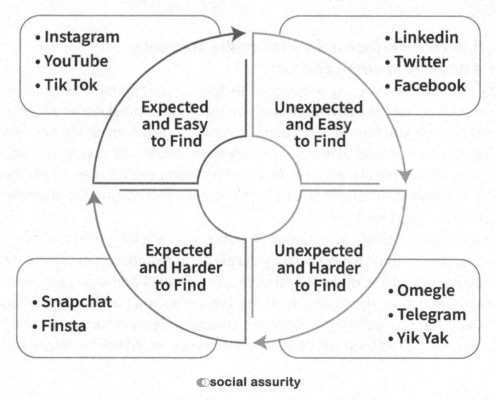

• Instagram
• YouTube
• Tik Tok

Expected and Easy to Find

• Linkedin
• Twitter
• Facebook

Unexpected and Easy to Find

Expected and Harder to Find

• Snapchat
• Finsta

Unexpected and Harder to Find

• Omegle
• Telegram
• Yik Yak

◉social assurity

In the competitive world of college admissions, applicants should be embracing social media to set themselves apart from other highly qualified candidates. Social media platforms provide college admissions officers a window to assess an applicant's credibility, maturity, authenticity, and even likeability. With applications surging at the nation's most competitive colleges and with the rise of test-optional and test-blind admissions, serious applicants should consider their digital presence as essential.

Many colleges have adopted a holistic approach toward student assessment, looking beyond GPA and test scores. Test-optional and holistic admissions review an applicant's whole academic and lived experience. Many schools are placing an increasing emphasis on personal qualities. This renewed focus on character includes examining curiosity, leadership, love of learning, perseverance, and grit.

Social media is one way of delivering this missing and actionable information to admissions, enrollment, and financial offices. Not only can social media positively impact acceptance and scholarship decisions by showing an applicant's readiness, abilities, skills, and character, but it can also be used to gauge an applicant's interest in a particular college.

Tip #4: Tether college-focused social media accounts to a dedicated email address.

Create a Gmail account using a recognizable form of your name. This email prefix should also become your college social media username (e.g., firstnamelastname@gmail.com = @firstnamelastname). If you have a very common name, consider including your middle name or middle initial as an additional identifier on all social media sites. This technique will lead colleges to discover the social media content students want them to see. In addition, this will help students increase their "Likelihood to Enroll" score by leveraging the algorithms measuring their digital activities (see Tip #8).

It is best practice to create a new email address specifically for college and career purposes. Due to email's unique nature, every social media platform requires users to validate their identity via a valid email address during registration. These email addresses are then given high priority in search function algorithms. By using the same email address for all social media registrations and for your college/employment correspondence, chances are very good that searches using this email address will deliver the results you would want colleges and employers to see.

Tip #5: Create new social media profiles specifically for college.

It is liberating to separate your social media activities with friends from the content colleges want to see (see Tip #3). Think about using less teen-centric platforms like LinkedIn, Twitter, or Facebook to build your college-facing digital presence. You can also establish separate accounts on Instagram. Create new social media accounts using the Gmail account created for college correspondence. And using the same name and photo on all social media platforms will make your profiles more recognizable.

Tip #6: Build a digital portfolio that showcases your strengths.

You can use social media to build visual portfolios that showcase your interest in your intended course of study. For example, graphic design, art history, architecture, or fashion.

In the previous chapter, we took a deep dive into building a compelling digital portfolio for college on LinkedIn. But students can also use YouTube, TikTok, and Pinterest as foundational social media platforms. Instagram is an excellent tool for students who want to present their portfolios to schools in dynamic ways. You can create two Instagram accounts: one for fun with your friends and the other to build a public portfolio for your future.

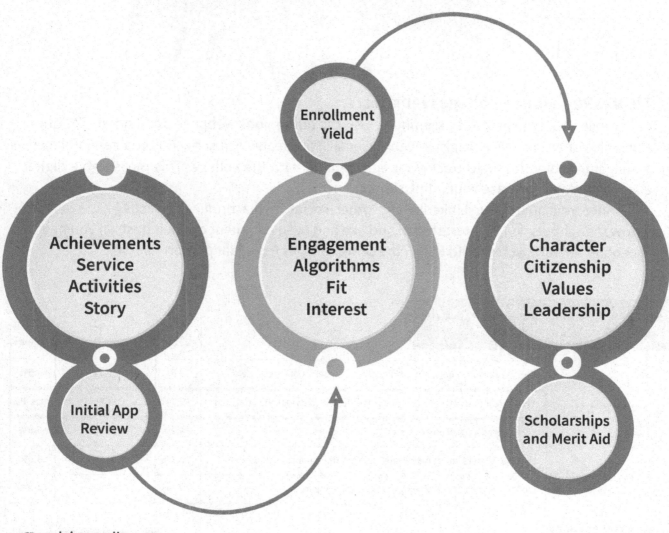

social assurity

Tip #7: Register on college websites.

Once your college list is assembled, visit the admissions webpage and find the "Request More Info" or a similar link. Register with the email you created in Tip #4. This enables enrollment management algorithms to track your engagement with the college. This measurable digital engagement will increase your admissions chances.

After you build your LinkedIn and other social media profiles for college, be sure to follow the schools you're interested in and like and even comment on their posts. If you have a Facebook account, you should follow the same colleges from that platform as well.

Student interest in particular schools is increasingly reflected in their interaction with those schools on social media

	2017	2019	Change
Every college and university should have a social media presence	79.6%	86.1%	+6.5%
The more interested I am, the more I interact with a school on social media	55.2%	74.6%	+19.4%
I discovered a particular college or university on social media	19.2%	25.8%	+6.6%
I used a school's social media site to link to the school's website	22.7%	29.6%	+6.9%
I follow school's that I am intereested in applying to	13.0%	17.8%	+4.8%

Percentage points

◐social assurity

Tip #8: Follow student social media ambassadors, student blogs, and college departments

Use your college-specific social media accounts to actively engage with a college's broader digital community. Most colleges are very active on Twitter, TikTok, and Instagram. Follow specific schools within the college, and then follow professors who teach at those schools.

Social media is a 24/7 communications tool that creates an enormous number of touch-points between applicants, colleges, and employers beyond the traditional application process. Social media's "social" aspect is all about engaging with others, which opens up a vast networking opportunity. And the "media" aspect of social media is all about creating content that authentically reflects one's aspirations, talents, commitment, and character.

Most schools use their websites to encourage students to connect with their social media channels. Why? By inviting prospective students to follow their social media feeds, colleges build a data-driven infrastructure for recruitment, assessment, and enrollment functions. By linking a student's name to a specific IP and email address, colleges can apply tracking pixels (tiny snippets of code that allow websites to gather visitor-identifying information) and other social listening tools to measure identified users' social media activities and website engagement. By evaluating this digital version of demonstrated interest, enrollment management algorithms can assign values to predict the likelihood that these applicants will enroll if accepted.

With colleges overtly beckoning prospective students to connect with them on social media, students need to be equipped with essential knowledge of how social media works and how colleges use collected data to make important decisions.

To truly understand the scope of college admissions today, you need to widen your perspective by getting familiar with enrollment management systems (which are today's true engines of college admissions) and merit aid decisions.

Colleges are increasingly turning to advanced enrollment management systems and enrollment consultancies to help them make better-informed decisions about prospects and applicants. Using big data algorithms, today's enrollment management systems are designed to monitor and measure an applicant's probability to enroll, ability to pay, and likelihood to graduate. Put simply, these tools create a predictive model. Student demographic data and online behavior — just like your own data and online behavior on Amazon, Twitter, Facebook, or Google — can be and is being mapped.

Big data and predictive analytics work best for both the college and the student when the system can connect applicants to their online activities. Almost all college enrollment management systems use the college website as the central hub to identify this critical base level. Website analytics routinely measure a visitor's browsing activities, such as page visits and time spent on each page. Unless visitors identify themselves by providing their name and email address, they often remain anonymous beyond their registered IP address.

Tip #9: Only follow, comment, and mention colleges from social media profiles created or curated specifically *for* colleges.

Students would not go to a college interview straight from the gym without first showering and changing their clothes. The same principle applies to social media. Students need to know that colleges see every mention of their names. Posts such as "I got accepted to X College but will go to Y College if accepted there" will be seen by both X and Y College.

Tip #10: Invite colleges to look at your curated social media profiles by including URLs within your applications.

When you embed your social media URL(s) within your college applications and invite admissions officers to learn more, you're increasing the chances that they will pay special attention to you. This is your opportunity to shine!

For years, we have been saying that when it comes to social media and college admissions, having nothing to hide is not the same as having something to show. So a natural question to ask is whether college admissions officers will look at social media if invited to do so by the applicant. Harvard's dean of admissions has already answered that question.

Excellent grades and academic rigor will always be the primary metric for college admissions. But a student's chances for acceptance will significantly improve once they properly utilize leverage media. Use platforms like LinkedIn to demonstrate interest, convey good character, and showcase the skills and personal attributes colleges are looking for.

> *If someone sends us a link of any kind, it doesn't have to be from some company or some organization, if it seems relevant to making the best possible case for that person's admission, we will certainly take a look at it.*
>
> *– WILLIAM FITZSIMMONS, Dean of Admissions, Harvard*

Here's What to Post

Once the accounts are created and the bios are written, it's time to start posting. Students can leverage social media to broadcast their authentic and best selves. And before clicking "publish," remember to put content through the PURE Test: Is it **P**ositive, **U**nbiased, **R**espectful, and **E**thical?

Below are just a few ideas of what you can publish:

College tours. Share pictures from a college tour you took.

Community activities. While you should include your involvement in community activities on your application, showing this through social media is quite another thing. For example, do you have photos collecting food and supplies for a local homeless shelter? Are you retweeting or reposting interesting articles about climate change?

News articles. Sharing a link to a news article with thoughtful comments on the topic shows leadership, critical thinking, and intelligent analysis.

Academic or extracurricular awards. You should note academic awards or positive recognition in your volunteer work or internships.

Here's What **NOT** to Post

Social media can help and hurt you in all stages of the admissions process. Just because you have your application sent in or have received an accepted offer does not mean you no longer need to exercise discretion on social media. This goes for posts or comments you may make within seemingly private groups. Consider what occurred when Harvard rescinded applications to ten students for negative social media behavior. Never trash-talk anything or anybody, be it a school you want to attend, teachers, or your supervisor at an after-school job. Admissions officers consider these comments a red flag. You wouldn't want to miss an internship or job opportunity because someone from the interview team felt that your TikTok or Instagram account was concerning.

SOCIAL MEDIA: RED FLAGS TO AVOID

Social media reflects your character. Avoid these behaviors at all costs so that your application isn't sent straight to the rejection pile:

- Offensive language
- Discriminatory comments
- Images of alcohol or drug use
- Illegal or illicit content
- Unprofessional usernames
- Negative comments
  (about school, previous jobs, etc.)
- Violence or bullying
- Confidential or sensitive information about people or previous employers
- Absence of a social media presence

Dress for Success

Let's log off for a moment and step back into the physical world. Always make sure your appearance matches the image you want to project. Find out what kind of clothes are appropriate for your personal brand and invest in the best you can reasonably afford. Err on the side of formality. Also, consider body language. The effectiveness of your Uniquely Me statement is not just based on what you say but how you say it.

You may be completely serious, passionate, and confident about what you have to say, but your body and clothing could be sending a different message. Image matters. When practicing and delivering your Uniquely Me statement, consider:

- Posture
- Eye Contact
- Volume
- Tone
- Facial expression
- Clothing
- Handshake

BRANDAMENTALS

Here are some top takeaways to deliver the best you have to offer:

1 **Don't hide online.** The goal isn't to evade college admissions officers on social media. It's to present your best self.

2 **Know the rules of social media.** Commit the fundamentals to heart, like that *posts never disappear* and *that people are always listening.*

3 **Engage with colleges' social media.** Follow your dream college's accounts, like their content, and make yourself seen.

4 **Post college-centric content.** Show admissions officers you really care by posting about your college tour, the topics you want to study, and more.

PART VII — NETWORKING FOR SUCCESS

You know what they say: *It's all in who you know.* People with solid professional networks have a career advantage. The key to future success is starting now and learning how to build an amazing network of connections that will help achieve your academic and career goals. Think of your network as your net worth.

The core of effective networking is solid, authentic relationships. It's best not to focus on how many people you meet networking. Instead, focus on meeting the *right* people. Quality, not quantity. Engage and build relationships with mentors, professors, industry leaders, and others. Relationships are built on trust, so make sure you deliver on your promise.

Expanding your network gives you the best chance of succeeding academically and professionally. Take the time to network strategically, consistently, and purposefully every day. Still not convinced? Consider the data:

- **85 percent of jobs are filled via networking. (HubSpot, 2019)**
- **80 percent of professionals consider networking a vital part of their career. (LinkedIn)**

The desire to fade into the woodwork and avoid engaging adults is a common teenage aversion. Get over it! You will often find that busy adults in high-ranking positions are receptive to questions from teens interested in their professions. As an example, if you are intrigued by 3D-CAD (three-dimensional computer-aided design), you can find online communities where experts are happy to mentor newbies. When you are ready to apply to engineering school, those same individuals are likely willing to write letters of recommendation.

Networking Basics

- **Start building social capital now.** Most students wait until they need a network to create one. But networking is not something you can cram in the night before. Networking is an art, and it takes time and energy to develop your skills. As an ambitious student, job seeker, or entrepreneur, it must be a part of your daily activities. Just like friendships, the most authentic and meaningful professional relationships develop naturally over time. Take note: If you have an early interest in a particular college, identify and connect with alumni as soon as possible rather than waiting until the eleventh hour.

- **Ensure all networking relationships are mutually beneficial.** Networking is not a "one-way street." Although you may feel you have nothing of value to offer more professional contacts, you never know how you may be able to help them. Simply asking if there's anything you can do for them shows that you are interested in building a relationship and willing to return the favor. Sharing connections, support, and resources with others is key.

- **Become comfortable introducing yourself.** Once you have clarity on who you are, it will be easier to communicate this to others. Consider how you would respond to the question, "Tell me about yourself"? Here's where you can apply your Uniquely Me statement and key messages. Be concise and project confidence. For example, James started a tutoring business and has an opportunity to meet parents at a local school event and promote his services. His pitch: "I'm a senior in high school who has five years of experience tutoring middle and high school students in math, and I plan to major in education in college. I'm passionate about making learning fun and adapting tutoring sessions to personal learning styles."

- **Be a strategic networker.** Having a game plan when networking will help you cover desired topics, establish professionalism, and gain credibility. Decide beforehand what you want to gain from networking, such as career exploration or making new connections. And regardless of your goal, always build rapport before making an ask. A good rapport goes a long way: When a potential opportunity arises in the future, your contact may be willing to refer you.

- **Be open to new experiences.** How do you make valuable connections? The solution: By saying "yes"! You'll be amazed at what happens when you say "yes" to opportunities like networking events (virtual and live), college info sessions, professional associations, extracurricular activities, and more. There are plenty of experiences online, too: Once your LinkedIn profile is complete, join groups that reflect your interests and skills.

- **Volunteer your talent and time.** The best way to make new connections is by getting out there and meeting people — and volunteering is a rewarding way to make new connections. Further, other volunteers and nonprofit staff can serve as potential sources of career advice and mentorship. You may even want to plan a community service/fundraising event that allows you to showcase your leadership skills.

- **Express gratitude.** Showing your appreciation is an essential element of professional networking. Send an email (or even better, a handwritten note) within one to two days to anyone who provides you with advice or ideas. Refer to the next page for a sample email:

- **Maintain relationships.** The best way to maintain a relationship is through consistent communication. After you meet a valuable contact, reach out to them within 48 hours while they are fresh in your mind. Here are a few ideas for staying in touch: Invite someone to an event you're attending. Comment on their recent social media posts. Send them a holiday or

Hi Lauren,
It was great meeting you at the career fair yesterday. I appreciate you taking the time to tell me about working at XYZ Company. I enjoyed learning how your career path evolved after graduation. I'm very interested in the summer internship program and plan on applying. I'll be sure to keep you posted on the outcome.
With gratitude, Sara

birthday card. Or share news of interest. You can always find a reason to follow up. In terms of frequency, it's ideal to reach out four to six times a year so that you are top of mind should an opportunity arise.

■ **Practice makes progress (not perfect).** Instead of striving for networking perfection, aim for improvement. "Practice makes perfect" sets people up for failure. Networking is a new skill set for teens, and it will likely feel awkward at first. However, practicing your Uniquely Me statement and key messages and exposing yourself to varied networking opportunities will build confidence. View everywhere as your practice arena — from the supermarket line to the career seminar to your cousin's graduation party.

EXERCISE: Building Out Your Network

This exercise will help you build and maintain a strong professional network. Fill out the names of people you know and trust in each of the following categories:

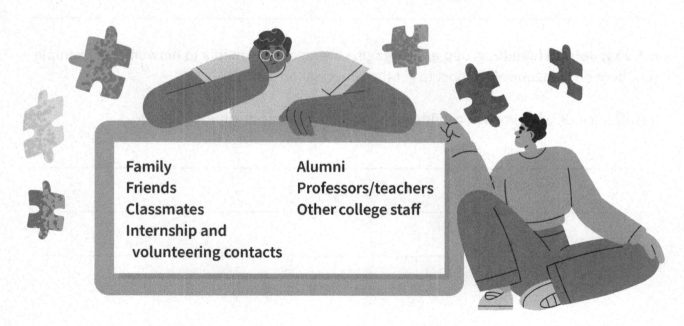

Family
Friends
Classmates
Internship and
  volunteering contacts

Alumni
Professors/teachers
Other college staff

Networking Activities

Complete the networking activities below and report back on your experience.

Activity: Strike up a conversation with a stranger. It could be waiting in the Starbucks line or waiting for a doctor's appointment. The conversation doesn't have to be lengthy — you could comment about the weather or an interesting piece of jewelry.

Result (Include what you felt confident about and any areas of improvement.)

_____

_____

_____

Activity: Videotape yourself for one minute to identify any speech tics (e.g., "um," "like") or if you have a nervous habit like fiddling your hair. Aim for a natural delivery that feels confident but not contrived.

Result (Include what you felt confident about and any areas of improvement.)

_____

_____

_____

Activity: Join a LinkedIn group and engage. Leverage social media to network. For example, comment on someone else's post to get the conversation started.

Result (Include what you felt confident about and any areas of improvement.)

_____

_____

_____

Activity: Attend an event related to your desired career, hobby, or interests, like a career seminar. Aim to meet two to three people and to follow up over email.

Result (Include what you felt confident about and any areas of improvement.)

_____

_____

_____

Activity: Meet people through other people. Reach out to one of your first-degree connections (people you are directly connected with) for a warm intro to a second-degree connection that would be meaningful for you to know.

Result (Include what you felt confident about and any areas of improvement.)

_____

_____

_____

Asking for an Introduction

Asking someone for an introduction can be intimidating. In fact, "Meet People Through Other People" was probably the most challenging activity for many. Whether exploring career options or seeking an internship, your existing network is often your most valuable asset for making connections. So how do we create these valuable connections? Let's take a deep dive into setting the stage for "introduction" success. Here are a few essentials:

■ **Pick the right contact.** It's best to choose a close friend, family member, or mentor to make an intro. Warm introductions are better received than cold outreach, but don't let that stop you from trying. The key is to find common ground, like the same school, interests, or employment. LinkedIn is one of the best sources to find out about a person's work, education, and interests.

- **Clearly state why you're requesting an intro.** Talk about why connecting to the particular person can help reach a specific goal (e.g., career exploration, job opening). For example: *Hi Cheryl, It was great seeing you last week at the football game. As you know, I'm actively looking for a summer internship and noticed that you are connected to Bill Anton, the internship program director for ABC Company, through LinkedIn. The ABC Company is top of my list of internship possibilities, and I'd appreciate an intro to Bill if you feel comfortable doing so. Many thanks for your support. Best, Nicole*

- **Make it easy for them to make the intro.** Give them a "plug and play" blurb to pass along to their contact. Your mutual contact will more likely comply if they don't need to put in a lot of effort and can simply copy, paste, and hit send. It also gives you the power to control the narrative. Let's take the above example and expand on it: *I know that you're busy with midterms and that this is a big ask, so I've included a short blurb to make the intro as easy as possible* (and, of course, feel free to edit as you see fit): *Hi Bill, My close friend and schoolmate Nicole Mann is very interested in your internship program…*

- **Don't forget "please" and "thank you."** Keep in mind that you are asking your contact to use some of their precious social capital, so make sure that you are polite and respectful with your ask. Also, remember that there is a chance that your contact may feel uncomfortable making the intro or not know the person well. Regardless of the outcome, thank your contact for their time and effort. And after your networking conversation, thank your introducer and let them know how it went.

- **Keep your message short and concise.** Aim for two to three sentences. Respond enthusiastically and remind the new contact of your mutual connection and why you are reaching out. Make sure to scan through their profile so you can share anything you have in common (e.g., went to the same summer camp, interests, etc.). Once you receive a response, it is appropriate to thank the introducer and move them to bcc (if you connect via email). Offer two to three specific dates and time ranges to meet up by phone, Zoom, or in person. Make sure they know you are flexible with their schedule and preferences. Once they confirm, send them a calendar invite.

- **Warming up a cold outreach.** Creating an eye-catching subject line will increase the chances of the message being opened. Equally important is customizing/personalizing your message. A generic invitation without a personal note is not the way to go; your chances of getting a response from a customized message are much higher. Add humor if that fits with your personality. Also, adding a question at the end of your message is an excellent technique to give the prospect a reason to respond.

**Example 1
(connection in common):**
*Hi Sally,
I noticed that we're both connected to Jeanne Morse. I also saw on your profile that we both interned at Company ABC.*

**Example 2
(no connection in common):**
Hi Max, I came across your profile after seeing your post about blockchain and real estate. I'm considering getting a certificate in real estate this summer and would love to learn more about the industry. It seems like it is a very fast-moving arena that would fit my personality well. Please let me know if you would be game to share some wisdom with me. Many thanks.

Striking up a conversation with a stranger — particularly in person — isn't easy. Don't get discouraged if your early attempts aren't home runs. And remember, not everyone is comfortable sharing their networks with others. Respect people's boundaries and the limits they are willing to go to help you. And remember, practice makes progress!

BRANDAMENTALS

Commit these top takeaways to memory:

1 **The core of networking is relationships.** Don't approach networking as simply transactional. It's only as successful as the depth of your relationships.

2 **Start building social capital now.** Teens shouldn't wait until they need a network to build one. Start early, so it's ready and waiting when the time comes.

3 **Don't be shy.** Fading into the woodwork and avoiding adults is common for teens. But get over it! Busy adults in high-ranking positions are often receptive to questions from teens interested in their professions.

4 **Practice makes progress (not perfect).** Networking is an art form that takes practice. Don't get discouraged if you're not hitting home runs during your first at bats.

PART VIII – WINNING THE COLLEGE ADMISSIONS GAME

As acceptance rates to selective schools plummet each year, the world of college admissions feels more competitive — and the margin of error slimmer — than ever before. So, what can you do to stand out from the ever-growing crowd?

Admissions officers spend an average of ten minutes per college application — which means teens need to make a **strong** impression fast. You need to consider which qualities admissions officers most value — leadership, determination, and dedication to public service — and incorporate them into your social media profiles. Don't leave admissions officers wanting more — catalog *all* your wins.

But don't take it from me. I scoured the globe to get tips from college admission officers and educational consultants to get their priceless insights on getting an edge in the college admission process. Read on.

40-Plus College Experts Weigh in on What Tips the College Balance to Acceptance

As a high school student, the college admissions process can feel overwhelming. As the college admission process becomes increasingly competitive, what gives students the leading edge? To get some insight, we asked over 40 college admission experts to weigh in on what they think are the most important factors in admission success.

Here's what they had to say.

Take a summer course at the college you want to attend. A lot of colleges have summer programs open to high school students. Attending one of these programs will not guarantee admission, but it will give you the experience of what it's like to go to that college. In addition to this, building connections at that specific school can be important when asking for recommendation letters or for people to help proofread your personal statement and scholarship applications. Finally, students should "vet" their social posts, including photos, through the lens of an admissions officer. Use your social profiles to showcase your best characteristics, and always be mindful of what you post online. If admissions personnel are looking, give them something positive to see.

James Lewis, President, National Society of High School Scholars (NSHSS), GA

■■■■■■■■■■■■■■■■■

To make a strong impression, establish an e-relationship with the admissions staff member who recruits in your region (you can typically find this person on the website). Ask thoughtful questions of that person — not simply questions for which the answers are easily available on the college website — and correspond perhaps several times a month. But don't overdo it! When it is time to visit, ask that person if you can make an appointment to see him/her, perhaps for an interview if they offer one. **The most important qualities of an applicant include academic performance and promise** — challenging oneself appropriately (tackling multiple AP classes and earning Cs does not reflect positively) with a strong curriculum through to senior year — and **personal qualities** — giving of oneself to help others, including family members, asking thoughtful questions and being engaged in the admission process. Don't just ask a teacher to write a reference; let them know why you think you are a good candidate for particular colleges.

Bob Massa and Bill Conley, Principals and Cofounders, Enrollment Intelligence Now, PA; Massa is VP for Enrollment Emeritus at Dickinson College; Conley is retired VP for Enrollment at Bucknell University. Both previously served as the Dean of Enrollment at Johns Hopkins University.

■■■■■■■■■■■■■■■■■

 real secret sauce is to intentionally transform the college process and experience into having deep meaning driven by purpose. Express your reason for choosing your major and why the college is right for you. Build upon your message, consistently delivering it to represent your authentic self. Never try to say what you think someone else wants to hear. Instead, focus on the message you would like others to know about you. The reality is that the student's academic record is used to determine if they are permitted to "enter the room." A stream of communications, including emails and Zoom calls, personalizes the process. Let's face it; it's easy to deny an electronic application. Students who humanize the process, expressing deep meaning for their life and defined purpose for college, are at a distinct advantage.

Hans Hanson, Founder and CEO, CollegeLogic, CT

■■■■■■■■■■■■■■■■■■

a student has built up an impressive social media following for one of their hobbies (such as a YouTube channel showcasing their musical talents), then that is a sign of their passion, which admissions officers look for. Admission officers want to create a well-rounded campus, which means they admit a class of specialists, each of whom brings unique talents, experiences, and viewpoints to the campus. Demonstrating your passion and commitment by diving deeply into one activity helps you stand out in the minds of admissions officers and shows what you care about. This doesn't mean you can't have a diverse set of extracurriculars merely that having a clear passion aids your chances of admission.

Antonio Cruz, Mentor, Ivy Scholars, TX

■■■■■■■■■■■■■■■■■■

 a member of the Character Collaborative, I believe it's important for students to demonstrate strong character attributes in the admission process. Colleges aim to admit students whose applications show desirable traits, including resilience, grit, empathy, kindness, service, compassion, open-mindedness, integrity, motivation, humility, and many others. These characteristics can become apparent to admission officers through their essays, interviews, teacher/counselor recommendation letters, and résumés/activity lists. I also advise students on social media etiquette, as it's essential that teens present their best selves. There should be no suggestion of alcohol consumption, suggestive photos, crude behavior, bullying, or inappropriate language. They shouldn't post anything they wouldn't want their parents to see.

Laurie Kopp Weingarten, CEP, President, One-Stop College Counseling, NJ

Personal branding and marketing are at the core of college admissions and athletic recruiting. Whether you're applying to college or looking to be recruited by a college coach, don't hesitate to show off a little (or a lot). Positively leverage social media. Social media is a living résumé that showcases your character. Don't miss out on an opportunity to share the latest A+ paper or creation from art class. Showcasing who you are, as well as your activities and interests, is something that colleges are looking for — make sure to impress them! They want more than just transcripts and an academic ace — they want someone who shows passion, is authentic, and will contribute positively to their campus. Post positively, publish proudly!

Chad Dorman, Founder, Leonard Andrew Consulting, CT

 most important characteristic a student can display is grit. The ability to persevere in the most difficult situations or to be able to thrive through the ups and downs of high school is something admission officers look for in college applications. It's the grit, the student's determination, and the ability to get up every time they fall that colleges value so much in their applicants (and eventually in their students). These demonstrated qualities that give college administrators confidence that even if a student is challenged at their college, they will not quit; instead, they will persevere and succeed (because they've done that in the past).

Anya Ilkys, Founder, College Starpoint, MA

Colleges have checked social media as far back as two years. Students should perform a strategic "social media audit" across all platforms they have used over the last two years. This includes evaluating posts, tags, and comments to determine if they reflect their values and character. Every social media platform should contain the same photo and public "about me" info so that colleges will be certain they have found the right person. After completing the audit, students can add to their digital footprint by regularly posting things that demonstrate their values. This may include motivational quotes, volunteer photos, and blog posts. For teens seeking scholarships, most are beginning the scholarship search too late, leaving money on the table. There are scholarships from kindergarten through professional school.

Denise Thomas, Founder, Get Ahead of the Class, FLA

As colleges build diverse classes of students with varied interests and backgrounds, students can stand out by deeply engaging in a specific interest or passion over a long period of time. Want to study business? It helps to start your own or have a job where you help run a business. Want to be in the tech field? Consider learning how to code, design websites, or build apps. Students who start exploring these interests early in high school (or even middle school) can have a leg up on the competition because the intended major they mark on their applications will match with how they spend their free time in high school.

Bradford Cake, Founder, Cake College Consulting, TX

■■■■■■■■■■■■■■■■■

Social media gets a lot of attention in the college admission (and job search) process, usually negative. However, some of my favorite adventures I have taken are when students provide a social media site that opens up an entirely new facet of who a student is. It is also a wonderful opportunity for us to see creative endeavors, activism, and engagement that might not be easily translatable to an application. For some students putting forth their social media profiles can be a game-changer for admission or scholarship opportunities. I love getting that insight into a student's life, one that is curated for their communities and peers — it is often one of the most authentic snapshots I will get of a student during the admission process.

Chloe Sigillito, Associate Director for Campus Visitation, Office of Undergraduate Admission, Fordham University, NY

■■■■■■■■■■■■■■■■■

Regardless of your privacy settings, it is safe to assume that anything you do online can be viewed by anyone, so conduct yourself accordingly. If there is something on your social media page that you do want the college to see, provide the link in your application. However, you can't assume that everyone reading your application will have the time to follow that link, so hedge your bets by including information about the project within the application itself. As an admissions counselor, the most important characteristics a student could show me were academic excellence, a passion for learning, a desire to have a positive impact, an ability to work hard and persevere, and a positive outlook on the world and those around them.

Carolyn Pippin, IvyWise, LLC; former Admissions Officer, TN

■■■■■■■■■■■■■■■■■

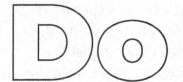**Do** your research. Colleges are as interested in what you can do for them as they are in what they can do for you. They want to know that you are a good fit for their mission, values, community and culture, and programs/offerings. Make sure you familiarize yourself with everything there is to know about the school — what programs they offer, how the football team performed last season, what their values are, who they favored for class president, who teaches what in your chosen major department, and so on. By talking about the school in specific, enthusiastic detail, you demonstrate that you are a good choice for joining its community.

Dr. Jen Harrison, Dissertation Coach, ReadWritePerfect, PA

■■■■■■■■■■■■■■■■■■

Admission officers and committees at selective institutions are accountable for building an incoming class of students that represents the school's values and culture. When making decisions between similar candidates, this can mean taking a look at applicants' social media profiles. A college admissions officer may check to see whether the applicant is following or engaging with other colleges, if what they share on social media aligns with the school's values and culture, and if their social media matches what they claim in their admissions essay.

Phil Ollenberg, Assistant Registrar, Bow Valley College, Canada

■■■■■■■■■■■■■■■■■■

Once in high school, students need to map out a general plan for their courses, extracurriculars, volunteering, employment, etc. The single biggest mistake is spreading themselves too thin. Colleges want smart, involved students with some level of focus on what's important to them, not students who are involved in a dozen activities at a cursory level. Colleges also want students who are willing to put others first and who share credit.

Pirie McIndoe, Founder, An Advisor for College, NC

■■■■■■■■■■■■■■■■■■

Students are often told that social media is a potential landmine in the college admissions process. However, social media can also be used as an advantage. For example, if a student has a particular interest, setting up an Instagram page or producing a series of TikTok videos can backstop expertise in a field. A Facebook page can shed light on a nonprofit or business a student has created. And many colleges have Twitter or Facebook accounts where students can show interest, get information, and potentially even interact with admissions officers who might be the very ones reviewing their applications.

Tira Harpaz, Founder, CollegeBound Advice, NY

■■■■■■■■■■■■■■■■

what very few others will; take college classes in high school, in person, at a respected school. The best way to show you will succeed in college is to have already had success at the college level. In addition, you're so ready for college, you've already started.

Clark Steen, Founder, Power Forward Tutoring, PA; former Admission Officer at Penn State

■■■■■■■■■■■■■■■■

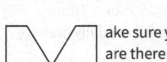ake sure you know a lot about the school. On the one hand, admissions officers are there to answer questions, but what's even better is to be well-researched enough to ask questions they don't hear typically. This shows that you are a critical thinker with good basic research skills and a work ethic. **Reach out to your local admissions representative** before your senior year or junior year. Let them become a part of your journey. Lastly, demonstrated interest matters in the college admission process. Creating a social media post customized to a school or engaging with the university's social media is a small but positive step that students can take.

Allen Koh, CEO, Cardinal Education, CA

■■■■■■■■■■■■■■■■

 your best self and don't take yourself too seriously. Humility, humor, and self-awareness scream understated confidence. It will be refreshing for the admissions officers to read an application that screams "AUTHENTIC!" Avoid overusing terms that are already popularized in the zeitgeist like "community," "diversity, equity and inclusion," and "social-emotional learning." These types of words make your essay sound like a copy-paste where you haven't done a self-reflective, objective deep dive. Remember, you want to be MEMORABLE. So be genuine, humble, mature, and self-deprecating.

Teru Clavel, Educational Consultant/Founder, Teru Consults, and Author, World Class, NY

 goal-oriented. Students can make a strong impression by having a well-rounded understanding of their academic and professional goals. Consider what experience you have in the field of study you are applying for. Some examples that can boost any college application are research experience, internships, awards, scholarships, volunteer work, tutoring, and more. Students who possess a strong desire to achieve their academic and professional goals demonstrate work ethic, dedication, and resilience. College life has its challenges as students become more independent and make their own decisions. Those students who demonstrate focus on their academic goals will be able to successfully manage their personal, academic, and professional demands.

Dr. Angedith Poggi, DHSc, MPH, Founder & Educational Consultant, Angedith Poggi, LLC, GA

ocial media is full of "glamour," which is not always authentic. Be honest and transparent. Applicants should highlight their accomplishments (academic and otherwise) and start engaging in meaningful conversations on topics they are interested in with those in the industry. Social media has changed the game in disseminating information for both institutions and potential students. Not only is information distributed instantaneously today, it also gives a deeper glance into the lives of applicants. Admission teams can see what an applicant does for fun, hobbies, life outside of school, and if the information included in an application or essay matches or contradicts what is on their social media feed.

David Clingenpeel, Associate Registrar, Wake Forest University; Former Admissions Officer at a Private University in Virginia, North Carolina

Social media has broadened the lens through which colleges view potential applicants. Students may cringe at the thought of admissions officers viewing their profiles to gain more insight, but they shouldn't. You can leverage social media in the admissions process in many ways. You are your best marketing tool. Be yourself, flaws and all. Don't try to create a caricature of who the admissions committee wants you to be. Just be mindful of public content that doesn't align with who you truly are. Use video to showcase your passions and skills. If interested in attending a university, follow and engage with them. Stay tuned in to be the first to know when events, activities, and deadlines are happening.

Robert Walker, High School Admissions Manager, University of Advancing Technology, AZ

■■■■■■■■■■■■■■■■■

 ability to clearly articulate to an admission committee, either in written words in an essay or verbally in an admission interview, what you will bring to the institution is critical. As the admission process becomes more opaque with the elimination of testing as a metric, students must demonstrate to the decision-makers why they are the best fit academically and socially. This can be done via strong application essays, solid recommendation letters, and a genuine interview experience.

Kristina L. Dooley, CEP, Founder & President, Estrela Consulting, OH

■■■■■■■■■■■■■■■■■

 can dramatically increase your chances of getting into an elite school with these two tips. First, choose your AP courses strategically. Take more AP courses than other applicants to the same university, start early (Grade 9), and show mastery in the subject by getting top grades. In most cases, shoot for a minimum of ten AP courses. The second tip relates to entrepreneurship. A strong applicant will generally have about three to five entrepreneurial roles in their profile. Admission officers look favorably at entrepreneurial leadership because it demonstrates that the student can articulate a vision and make things happen. Our students have launched mobile apps, charity initiatives, viral petitions, YouTube channels, podcasts, an artificial intelligence club, a gender equality club, and more. Your goal should be to create something unique that lets you stand out from the rest.

Jamie Beaton, CEO and Founder, Crimson Education; Author, Accepted! NY

■■■■■■■■■■■■■■■■■

Admissions officers are looking for self-directed, trailblazing kids who can turn their passions into impactful projects. Launching and scaling a nonprofit or business venture in high school is probably the best way to stand out in the admissions process. This shows you're capable of creating and developing your own impactful project and have the potential to shine on campus. Entrepreneurship is not limited to founding, managing businesses, and taking risks; it involves finding solutions to problems and filling gaps in innovative ways. Conveying this through coherent branding and storytelling across multiple platforms (social media, interviews, etc.) is critical in this highly competitive process. Whether interested in art or astrophysics, students benefit by becoming entrepreneurs or thinking like one. A bonus tip: Secure validation and gain third-party recognition (e.g., media coverage, testimonials) and then showcase that on social media.

Pierre Huguet, PhD, CEO and Founder, H&C Education, MA

■■■■■■■■■■■■■■■■■

Students need to take control of their personal narratives and message. A common mistake students make is presenting everything they have done without taking the time to consider how everything fits together. Essays, activities, courses, and recommendations in their applications are presented as separate pieces. All these pieces need to come together to paint a complete picture and strong case for the student's background. What drives the student? How will they fit into the school's community? Students should get crystal clear about their passions and strengths. Whatever the student's narrative, it should demonstrate academic curiosity and be authentic. Social media should be consistent with their narrative and provide more context and depth.

Laura Perretta, PhD, Founder, Advanced Ivy Prep, IL

■■■■■■■■■■■■■■■■■

Many applications allow you to share web pages about yourself. If you are a high school journalist or a creative writer who has an archive of stories, sharing a website of such work can highlight your accomplishments and dedication over a longer period. Make sure not to use these spaces to repeat what is in your application but rather expand on what was shared. Don't try to be something you aren't during the admission process. You want to be at a college that is a good fit for you, where you will thrive both academically and socially.

Keri S. Bahar, Founder, KSB College Consulting, IL

■■■■■■■■■■■■■■■■■

 mindful of how you present yourself on social media. A single inappropriate post could disrupt your academic and professional trajectory. Fill your social media pages with strengths and skills. Share your accomplishments; tweet a link to a school newspaper article you wrote or Instagram a photo of you finishing a race. To demonstrate your preparedness and commitment to the school, conduct thorough research on programs (majors/minors), classes, student organizations, study abroad opportunities, and school traditions. This information will allow you to answer questions regarding your potential contribution and interest in the school; it will also empower you to ask insightful questions during an interview!

Nikki Geula, Founder and CEO, The Classroom Door, NY

■■■■■■■■■■■■■■■■■■

Ultimately, the candidate's application must answer the question, "Why me?" Why should the college pick that student over all the other seemingly equally qualified students (e.g., good grades, good test scores, good letters of recommendation)? The answer is that the student needs to stand out in some way. No employer will hire a student because she/he wrote a killer essay as a high school senior. However, if a student publishes scientific papers, writes a book, or starts a successful business, those accomplishments stay on their résumé for a lifetime.

John Leddo, PhD, Founder MyEdMaster LLC, VA

■■■■■■■■■■■■■■■■■■

Colleges want to learn about what makes a student unique. In this age of test-optional, colleges are doing a more holistic review of applications. Students need to ensure that each component of the application shines the best possible light on what makes them great. Social media presents an excellent opportunity to inter-act and share what strengths students will bring to campus. High school is an ideal time to begin professionally connecting and growing a network. Students should proactively engage with colleges of interest on LinkedIn or Twitter and like and comment on colleges' posts and updates.

Diane Steiger, Founder & Educational Consultant, Matrix College Consulting, OH

■■■■■■■■■■■■■■■■■■

Colleges are aware that life has been very different over the past few years. Admission officers do not want to hear about what students could not do, but rather what students accomplished despite (and even because of) the recent challenges. Students should demonstrate that they are active agents of change in their own lives and the lives of others. Taking a coding course, learning a new language, forming a neighborhood organization, or volunteering in the community are all examples of how students can make a unique and genuine difference. While grades and standardized test scores are still accepted on most university applications, the emphasis on these marks has decreased. Students can show their aptitude by enrolling in enrichment classes, earning certificates in specialized skills, and starting new intellectual hobbies.

Lindsey Wander, Founder, WorldWise Tutoring LLC, IL

■■■■■■■■■■■■■■■■■

Here are my top three tips for showing admissions officers who you are: (1) The most important aspect of the application is your essay, which turns you from a set of numbers into a human. The essay is a showcase of your particular self — what makes you you — helping them understand you as a person; (2) The best essay has a formula: Tell me about who you were, what event created a change in you, and who you became as a result. This evolution is not only interesting but shows your potential for growth; and (3) Any part of the application that's marked optional — do it! Consider it mandatory; the more information the admissions team knows about you, the better your chances of being accepted.

Alyssa Bowlby, Co-founder and Executive Director, Yleana Leadership Foundation, NY

■■■■■■■■■■■■■■■■■

A student preparing for auditions/interviews for music schools shared that one of her passions outside of music was baking. She had started her own gourmet baked goods company but was hesitant to share this in applications or interviews. I encouraged her to highlight this impressive accomplishment as it shows so much about her beyond her musical ability — and illustrated her personality, motivation, and capacity for achievement. She conceded and enthusiastically shared her business venture, which revealed many positive character traits. And, for the record, she was accepted at every institution she applied to, some of which were very competitive!

Dr. Christine Gangelhoff, Independent Educational Consultant and Professor of Music, University of The Bahamas, Bahamas

■■■■■■■■■■■■■■■■■

Universities raised the bar just when students thought good grades and impressive test scores were sufficient. Students' character has emerged as an essential determiner. Universities filter the top applicants using rigorous metrics beyond your academic and cocurricular abilities. Students need to build a strong profile, write a deft application, and create an impressive social media presence to vault ahead of the competition. Rather than relying on what your school offers in extracurricular activities. Explore the broader world and seek opportunities that are aligned with your values. Recommendation letters are a great way to impress, so invest the time to secure the strongest letters from the best sources. Lastly, put your best step forward on LinkedIn and follow suit for all other social media platforms.

Ashish Fernando, Founder and CEO, iSchoolConnect Technologies, India

■■■■■■■■■■■■■■■■■■

College hopefuls can stand out with videos that showcase their qualities and talents. For instance, a student who loves to volunteer could record a brief vlog that takes viewers on the journey of a volunteer project. Similarly, a student who plays for the band or a sports team can compile behind-the-scenes clips. This will demonstrate a more casual and "fun" side of the student. Personality makes a difference, and admission officers will take note!

Jessica Bonner, Founder, For Other Prizes Consulting, AL

■■■■■■■■■■■■■■■■■■

 key to making a strong impression in college admissions is to give admission boards insight into who you are as a person, not just the scores on paper. Often students spend countless hours trying to improve their test scores and GPAs. While it is important to have a solid GPA and test scores, time may be better spent on incremental improvements elsewhere. Students get a leading edge in colleges by participating in extracurriculars that demonstrate unique skills and passion. Students should focus on taking extracurriculars to the next level and impacting their local community.

Kristen Moon, Founder, Moon Prep, GA

■■■■■■■■■■■■■■■■■■

Students should spend more time than they think on their essays, which is their only chance to differentiate themselves from the crowd. The essay is the admission officer's first chance to meet you, so make it sound like the way you naturally speak. One student wrote about a "picture-perfect" volunteer opportunity where he tutored underprivileged kids in STEM. It sounded cliché, and he struggled with highlighting specific details. I dug deeper and found out that much of his free time is spent assisting his younger brother with autism. Multiple examples of daily family life showcased a love for his brother that didn't come across as trying to impress. This switch in topic showed his love of family, leadership, and creativity in a natural way that no official volunteer opportunity could.

Yelena Shuster, Founder, Admissions Essay Guru, TheAdmissionsGuru.com, NY

■■■■■■■■■■■■■■■■■■

Colleges want to make sure applicants are a good investment. Uniqueness is the most essential characteristic to have when applying. Make sure you stand out by getting involved in something cutting-edge or relevant. You want to be the application that the admissions officer talks about at the dinner table that night. Invest your time in unique niche organizations that match your selected major. Find or start programs that showcase your talents and what you plan to do during and after college. If you have not started something on Compass, such as creating a club, find something you can do in your community to solve a problem. Schools are looking for leaders and go-getters. There are many ways to do this, both in person and virtually.

Esmeralda Archer, Founder, Studypage Tutoring, CA

■■■■■■■■■■■■■■■■■■

Above all, be engaged. Be present and committed to your learning opportunities. Top colleges admit students devoted to a lifelong love of learning inside and outside of the classroom. Your extracurricular involvement should reveal your leadership and genuine interest in all the communities you help build. What does it mean to be engaged? In the end, you decide. Resist the urge to join causes you do not feel connected to for the sake of a longer résumé. Ask yourself: why am I choosing this class or extracurricular opportunity? When did my interest in the topic begin? How much time will I happily devote to this responsibility? How do I imagine that I can use the skills I learn in the future? In short, know your "why" and lead with joy and curiosity.

Racquel Bernard, Master Admissions Counselor, H & C Education; Former Assistant Director of Admissions, Dartmouth College, MA

Colleges use a lot of words to talk about what they are looking for in students. We want students who have demonstrated that they want to learn, stretch, and challenge themselves and others. We are attempting to build a community of students who have and will continue to invest in and influence people and things around them for the better. Ultimately, we want good high school students who will be missed by their schools and communities when they graduate.

Rick Clark, AVP and Executive Director, Undergraduate Admissions, Georgia Institute of Technology; Coauthor Truth about College Admission: A Family Guide to Getting In and Staying Together, GA

■ ■ ■ ■ ■ ■ ■ ■ ■ ■ ■ ■ ■ ■ ■ ■ ■ ■

By developing a personal brand, students learn about themselves and how to present their values, interests, talents, and skills to the world through the ever-changing social media and digital world! Best method to teach students the importance of their online footprints and how to use tools that will help them best market their authentic selves. Not only helpful in the college admissions process, but for a student's future professional career!

Karen Memmelaar-Siegel, High School College Advisor, North Broward Preparatory School, FL

■ ■ ■ ■ ■ ■ ■ ■ ■ ■ ■ ■ ■ ■ ■ ■ ■ ■

 refreshing when we hear from students, whether to answer questions or to "meet" them in person, through email, video, or phone. Since there can be a long time between applying and getting a decision, updates can help a candidate stand out. When something new or noteworthy happens, or even if a college starts to become a more exciting option as you learn more or visit, you can pass that along to your admissions counselor as a way to stand out. Just make sure to not check in TOO often — once or twice is enough! Everyone has an opportunity to present themselves as a unique and multifaceted person through the admissions process. Beyond numbers, we want to know that the people we admit will be overall good campus citizens. What kind of roommate will they be? What groups will they contribute to? Openness, leadership, respect, energy, excitement, resiliency, and curiosity are all qualities that are positive elements of an application.

Sarah Bombard, Senior Associate Director, Lehigh University, Office of Admissions, PA

■ ■ ■ ■ ■ ■ ■ ■ ■ ■ ■ ■ ■ ■ ■ ■ ■ ■

Although a campus visit is likely the most impactful way to demonstrate interest, students don't necessarily have to invest in traveling across the country prior to learning an admission decision from their top college choices. Due to clever technology, colleges can track a student's interest and engagement through email, social media, and website traffic. To get a leading edge, students should open emails from colleges that interest them, click on the links or submit forms that provide more details about their interests and activities. Spend some time on the school's website after following a link from an email or text. Students can also take advantage of the robust virtual offerings, including live information sessions, student panels, or virtual interviews.

Jennifer Winge, VP for Enrollment, College of Wooster, OH

■■■■■■■■■■■■■■■■■■

To round out our discussion on how to craft a winning application, I spoke with Dr. Angel B. Pérez, CEO of the National Association for College Admission Counseling (NACAC) and former Vice President for Enrollment and Student Success at Trinity College.

While it may be tempting to pursue whatever you think "looks good" on a college application, Dr. Pérez recommends avoiding anything that isn't true to your real passions. Instead of trying to game the system and join the trend of the moment, you should spend your high school years developing your own authentic talents.

Admissions officers can tell when you're doing something for the application rather than for yourself. One dead giveaway? A padded activities list shows neither advancement nor long-term dedication. It's more impressive to hold the same no-frills tutoring job for all four years of high school as that displays work ethic and dedication — qualities admissions officers seek in their student body.

The best advice is to pursue activities that you are passionate about. "These days, there's so much overpreparing in the college admission process. You can easily tell when an app is not authentic and just reads like an adult has had a heavy hand," Dr. Pérez says.

He notes one such example from his years managing admissions at Trinity. There is a myth that Ivy League institutions want you to save the rainforest in Costa Rica. These service trips abroad have become clichés highlighting more about your family's ability to sponsor such a summer than your actual commitment to environmental science.

Similarly, beware of familiar essay tropes that may sound good on paper but don't represent who you are. Common anecdotes from your everyday life can be more effective than some grand story about traveling in Europe (especially if it's on your family's dime). One of Dr. Pérez's favorite essays during his time at Trinity was about a student working at a coffee shop — no fancy life story, just a "beautiful reflection on lessons learned," he says.

Be mindful of sounding like yourself when writing the essay. Don't try to use a thesaurus or be tempted to ask for your parents' help. "We can tell a mile away what a polished college application looks like," says Dr. Pérez. "While it's ok to let a few people review it, students should be selective in how many people see it. The more people you show your application to, the more you lose your voice in the process."

On the topic of social media, Dr. Pérez wants every student to ask themselves two "burning questions" regarding their online profiles. One: "If I were to look at your social media account right now, would you be embarrassed?" And two: "Would you want this person to be your roommate?" If the answer is no for either, you need to scrub your social media presence. And this is precisely the essence of the book — using social media to your advantage.

BRANDAMENTALS

Now, it's your turn to create the Brandamentals. What are your takeaways from this section? Did one of the college advisors' tips strike a chord? Please record below:

1. _____

2. _____

3. _____

PART IX — THE ENTREPRENEUR IN YOU

For some, entrepreneurship may just be your jam. I know it is for me! I grew up in a very entrepreneurial family. My parents had successful businesses in the fashion industry and, later, in real estate. I've always been a risk-taker and love to confront new challenges. I started my first business at age 14 — a home waitress service — with my friend Jen. Driven to make more than the standard hourly babysitting rate, we placed an ad in the local newspaper with the headline: *We Set, Serve & Clean Up. Let us help you at your next party.* The only expense was the purchase of a white uniform, bought second-hand. We ended up increasing our earnings by 500 percent, and we were booked for months with repeat business.

The lesson behind this story? Business success can be achieved at any age. And learning the fundamentals of business early has big advantages. You can use these skills — like time management, writing a business plan, creativity, and networking — in a wide variety of careers, classes, and life experiences. People with entrepreneurial mindsets can always fall back on their capabilities as self-starters rather than relying on a specific career path or employer.

Remember: "Entrepreneur" can mean different things to different people. To some, it might conjure up images of Silicon Valley billionaires who started their own tech companies in their garages. To others, it might be someone who owns a mom-and-pop shop down the street. Contrary to popular belief, entrepreneurship is not about having a million-dollar idea. It's about having the passion and perseverance to turn that idea into a reality. It's about being your own boss. And it's about building something from the ground up.

Of course, teens who wish to start a business should consult their parents or guardians first. If you are under eighteen, you are considered a minor and cannot form a legal business entity in the US. But adults can file on behalf of minor children. Since there are considerations (e.g., tax laws, contracts, bank accounts) that vary by state, your parents should consult with a trusted advisor like an attorney or CPA to determine which rules apply where you live.

Teen entrepreneurship is on the rise. The pandemic was a catalyst for a surge of business start-ups among teens. The combination of changing customer demands, e-commerce growth, and more flexible schedules have made it easier and more desirable to start a business.

Entrepreneurship by the Numbers

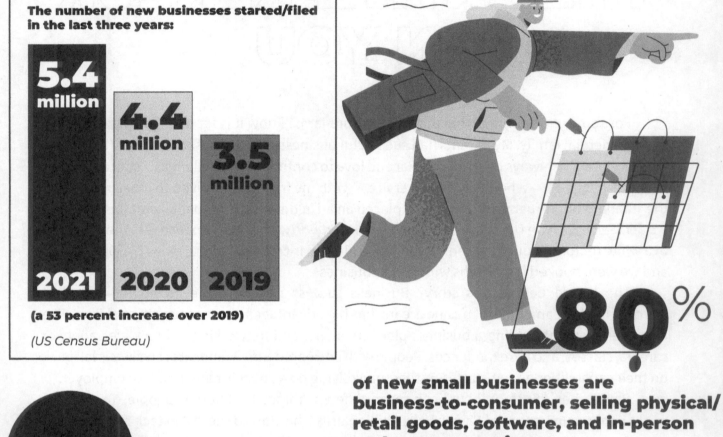

The number of new businesses started/filed in the last three years:

5.4 million — **2021**

4.4 million — **2020**

3.5 million — **2019**

(a 53 percent increase over 2019)

(US Census Bureau)

80% of new small businesses are business-to-consumer, selling physical/retail goods, software, and in-person and remote services.

(Salesforce 2021 Survey)

800,000 entrepreneurs in the US.

(Statista)

582 million entrepreneurs across the globe.

(GEM: Global Entrepreneurship Monitor)

70% of new businesses are born out of technology or tech-focused, and 25 percent of those surveyed said their business is purely digital, like app development.

(Salesforce 2021 Survey)

Around **20**% of small businesses fail in their first year.

(US Small Business Administration)

12.3 million women own their own businesses in the US

(WBENC: Women's Business Enterprise National Council)

70% of US businesses are women-owned.

Why Entrepreneurship?

- Creating new businesses is essential for a thriving economy and job creation.
- Small businesses are the most significant source of new jobs and economic growth in the US.
- New and disruptive services, products, or technologies created by entrepreneurs enable new markets to be developed and new wealth to be created.
- Entrepreneurs spark social change, which enhances the quality of life.
- Allows you to monetize your passion.
- Solves real, complex problems through innovation.
- Teaches life skills like public speaking and time management.
- Develops self-confidence, problem-solving abilities, and resourcefulness.
- Boosts your college-admissions profile and allows you to stand out.
- Allows you to be your own boss. The perk of owning your business is independence.

"BE A PROBLEM SOLVER, NOT A PROBLEM SPOTTER"

Entrepreneur Top Traits

So, you want to be an entrepreneur? Do you have what it takes? The entrepreneurial bug bites many young people, and for good reason. Starting your own business can be a gratifying experience. But what exactly does it take to be a successful entrepreneur? There's no one-size-fits-all answer to this question, but certain traits are common among successful entrepreneurs. Whether you're interested in starting your own business or want to become more entrepreneurial in your current job, read on for a quick overview of some essential attributes of successful entrepreneurs:

Grit – Perseverance and determination to see ideas through, no matter how hard things get. In the face of failure, resilience is key.

Risk-Taker – The ability to stretch out of your comfort zone and confront challenges head-on.

Passion – A burning desire to turn an idea into reality.

Flexibility – The ability to adapt to change. As the business and market shift, you have to go with the flow.

Creativity – Ability to think big and live in a state of curiosity to develop new ideas and innovative solutions.

Networker – As they say, your network is your net worth. Building relationships helps uncover opportunities, strategic partnerships, and new clients.

Purpose – Clarity on what you stand for. Commitment to your purpose needs to be steadfast.

Resourcefulness – The ability to make the most of what you have and get things done with limited resources. This often means optimizing your existing resources and doing more with less.

Many people think that only a certain type of person can be an entrepreneur, but this is not the case. Anyone can become a successful entrepreneur as long as they are determined and willing. Just make sure you have a solid plan in place to help you stay on track. So, what steps will you take today to begin your journey toward entrepreneurship success?

Entrepreneurship Programs for Teens

There is a growing trend to teach entrepreneurship in high school. What if you could learn the basics of starting a business before you even graduate? Or perhaps launch your own business? Sounds pretty amazing, right? Don't fret if your high school does not offer an entrepreneurship program — there are several other programs that can meet your interests and needs.

Many of these programs provide students with the opportunity to develop their business ideas, turn them into tangible products or services, and receive mentorship from local businesses and entrepreneurs. In some cases, students are even offered funding to launch their companies. Here are a few examples:

Spike Lab   www.spikelab.org

The six-stage Spike Incubation program coaches students through successfully building and launching a "Spike" — a meaningful project with a societal impact. A Spike must be "uniquely impressive," meaning it aligns with a student's personal background and interests. The project must also have a "real-world impact." Students have launched Spike projects ranging from urban beekeeping to youth robotics programs for inner-city kids. All students begin with a 12-week Starter Package consisting of weekly coaching sessions to create a solid foundation for their Spike. Following the completion of the Starter Package, the curriculum is fully customizable and offers multiple options (e.g., on-demand, weekly sessions). **Fee-based**

Whatever It Takes (WIT)　　　　　　　　　　www.doingwit.org

WIT is a nonprofit that provides training for teens to learn entrepreneurship and leadership skills through the design, launch, and growth of a social enterprise. WIT offers nine-month **college-credit classes** for high-school students in San Diego, New York City, Austin, and St. Louis. They also provide a more intensive program: Camp WIT, a weeklong virtual entrepreneur boot camp for teens that culminates in a pitch competition with $1,000 in cash prizes. The Do WIT program also hosts one-day hackathons, allowing teens to tackle real problems and pitch solutions to city officials, CEOs, entrepreneurs, and leaders. **Fee-based**

Junior Achievement　　　　　　　　　　　　www.ja.org

Junior Achievement (JA) is the world's largest nonprofit organization dedicated to helping students understand the importance of entrepreneurship, managing money, and preparing for college or a career. Through the delivery of innovative, experiential learning in work readiness, entrepreneurship, and financial literacy, JA gives students an advantage by providing real-world experiences not taught in schools. JA reaches over three million students nationwide in classrooms, after-school locations, and online. Programs are delivered by corporate and community volunteers who serve as the organization's backbone. JA Connect Entrepreneurship™ is a self-guided, on-demand learning resource featuring a flexible, modular repository of activities for the aspiring entrepreneur. **Free**

Juni Learning　　　　　　　　　　　　www.junilearning.com

Juni is an online platform that offers private, one-on-one, on-demand courses with access to an unlimited library and boot camps for specific skills and topics. The program is designed for grades six through 12, and representative topics include STEAM, coding, investing, storytelling, and more. Juni carefully matches students with instructors based on personality, skill set, and teaching style. The program features top US university instructors, project-based coursework, live support, instructor office hours, Juni Community (clubs, events, shared projects), and certificates of completion. **Fee-based**

Endevvr　　　　　　　　　　　　　　　　www.endevvr.com

Endevvr is a start-up incubator for high school students. The virtual, six-week summer program is a top-ranked entrepreneurship program held at Georgia Tech. They provide a highly interactive learning environment that enables students to create an actual company while building resilience, emotional intelligence, and advanced business skills. Mentorship and guidance are provided throughout the program. Student participants work closely with Georgia Tech faculty and other leaders to start and fund actual companies. **Fee-based**

BETA Camp

www.beta.camp

BETA Camp is a six-week online summer program that focuses on teaching high school students how to build a business from scratch. The program provides students with skills to design, test, and create a start-up that solves real customers' problems. The curriculum is taught by a team of industry professionals who bring their own unique experiences working at the forefront of innovation. The program features regular check-ins, group discussions, and workshops. By the end of the program, students will have built a working business. **Fee-based**

The Spaceship Academy

www.thespaceship.org

The Spaceship Academy is on a mission to educate aspiring change-makers worldwide by providing the tools they need to make a difference. The dynamic program offers various self-paced online courses that bridge social impact, sustainability, entrepreneurship, design thinking, and personal development to tackle some of the world's biggest social and environmental challenges. Participants get access to The Changemakers Playbook, which has a robust video library and other resources. The Spaceship Academy also features The Youth Innovation Challenge, which is open to high school students from 13–18 years old. Finalists receive a full scholarship to be part of the Spaceship's Impact Accelerator program; the winner is awarded a $1,000 cash prize. **Fee-based**

LaunchX

www.launchx.com

Launch X is one of the most widely known entrepreneurship summer programs, bringing together top aspiring high school entrepreneurs from around the world each summer. Launch X is a highly selective four-week program based on the MIT campus that equips students with the skills, resources, and innovative thinking to launch a start-up. Students work in a cohort with industry experts to solve problems and take their products from idea to execution. Teens gain insight into the secrets of running a business through workshops and notable guest speakers. The summer program is offered virtually and on various campus locations. **Fee-based**

Leangap

www.leangap.org

Leangap is an intensive six-week summer program that empowers high school students to build their own scalable companies and nonprofits. The program was established in 2015 by entrepreneur Eddy Zhong at age seventeen when he saw the need for formal entrepreneurship programs for high school students. Leangap helps students bring their ideas to life, from concept to successful launch, with resources from business leaders and top institutions. The Leangap curriculum takes student-run companies through market research, validation, feasibility, prototyping, beta testing, and fundraising. There are two session options to start early or late summer. **Fee-based**

University Startups

www.university-startups.com

University Startups provides innovative, entrepreneurship-focused curriculum and ground-breaking technologies to help students achieve their goals of attending college, starting a business, or finding a job. The program has been designed by expert instructors from top-tier universities and aims to remove barriers to college preparation, admissions, financial aid, internships, and career-path employment. A monthly subscription includes unlimited access to courses, virtual counseling, and admission to their Ambassador program. University Startups also work directly with educational institutions and nonprofits to provide customizable enriched college preparation and career programs. **Fee-based**

Babson Summer Study

www.babson.edu/admission/
visiting-student-program

Babson Summer Study is a four-week virtual entrepreneurial program for rising high school juniors and seniors to gain exposure to key entrepreneurship, management, marketing, finance, business communication, and other disciplines. Upon completion, students earn four college credits from Babson, a top-ranked college for entrepreneurship. The summer program features Babson instructors and guest speakers. Participants work closely with peers and mentors to create an entrepreneurial action plan. The goal? To launch a business and pitch it to the Babson community. **Fee-based**

Young Entrepreneurs Academy (YEA!)

www.yeausa.org

YEA! is a seven-month program that transforms middle and high school students into real-life entrepreneurs and business owners. Students learn how to generate business ideas, create a business plan, conduct market research, pitch to a panel of investors, and launch their own company. The program also features a CEO roundtable event, investor panel, trade show, guest lectures, and field trips to local businesses. YEA has helped over seven thousand students launch over 5,100 companies. One alumnus of the program has generated over $1 million in sales. **Fee-based**

Membership programs

Below are some membership groups that prepare students for careers in business. These national organizations have a network of chapters across the US and rely on dues to support program development, training, resources, technology, and events. Nominal annual membership dues vary by state (typically less than $100). If your high school doesn't have a chapter, be entrepreneurial and start one!

Future Business Leaders of America (FBLA)   www.fbla-pbl.org

FBLA is a student organization that helps high schoolers prepare for careers in business through academic competitions, leadership development, and educational programs. FBLA focuses on six areas to help students become successful business leaders: leadership development, academic competitions, educational programs, membership benefits, community service, and awards and recognition.

DECA   www.deca.org

DECA is a nonprofit organization that has high school chapters worldwide. The program helps students become college- and career-ready by providing marketing, finance, hospitality, and management skills. One of DECA's highlights is its competitive events. Students participate in various contests based on their interests, such as writing business plans, role-playing in business scenarios, and traveling to competitions and academic conferences. DECA members can also apply for state and national scholarships.

Business Professionals of America (BPA)   www.bpa.org

BPA is the leading CTSO (Career and Technical Student Organization) for students pursuing careers in office administration, business management, health administration, finance, information technology, and other related fields. BPA's showcase program, the Workplace Skills Assessment Program (WSAP), prepares students to succeed and assesses real-world business skills and problem-solving abilities. With over 45 thousand members in chapters located throughout 25 states and Puerto Rico, BPA hosts more than 90 competitive events for students to demonstrate their career skills at regional, state, and national conferences.

School- and community-based programs

Some programs are offered right in your community or school. Here are just two of them:

Uncharted Learning
www.unchartedlearning.org

Uncharted Learning is a nonprofit organization that helps schools and districts provide entrepreneurship programs to students in over three hundred schools across the US, Australia, and Spain. Uncharted Learning's year-long INCubatoredu program allows students to develop their own businesses and connect with industry professionals and culminates in a *Shark Tank-style pitch* event for potential funding. A second-year program, acceleratoredu, helps students launch their start-ups. Uncharted Learning has been named to the Inc. 2021 Best in Business list in the Youth Entrepreneurship category.

Network for Teaching Entrepreneurship (NFTE)
www.nfte.com

NFTE is a global nonprofit organization that provides high-quality entrepreneurship education to middle and high school students from under-resourced communities. NFTE has educated more than a million students through in-school, out-of-school, college, and summer camp programs. The curriculum is offered in person and online, reaching 25 states and 20 additional countries. Students create an original business idea, write a business plan, and vie for scholarships and seed capital at an annual business plan and pitch competition. NFTE boasts a robust volunteer network of entrepreneurs and successful businesspeople to support classroom activities. Summer Discovery, in partnership with *Inc. Magazine*, offers a unique entrepreneurship experience powered by the NFTE curriculum. **Free** (with the exception of the Summer Discovery program)

Fun Facts About Entrepreneurship

Did you know that some of the world's most famous entrepreneurs, like Bill Gates and Steve Jobs, started their businesses as teenagers? Building your own business can be a lot of fun, but it also requires hard work. Entrepreneurship is all about taking risks. And what could be riskier than stepping out on your own and starting a business? But for those who are daring enough, the rewards can be significant. If you're thinking of launching a business or curious about what it involves, read on for some inspiring entrepreneurship stories and tips. You never know — you might be the next Richard Branson or Oprah Winfrey!

Most successful entrepreneur. Tesla executive Elon Musk is currently the wealthiest entrepreneur, worth $223 billion (as of February 2022). Jeff Bezos, who started Amazon in 1994 to sell books, is worth $178 billion (as of February 2022).

Entrepreneurs who started in a garage. 12 companies worth more than $1 billion were founded in garages, including many tech companies but also Mattel, Maglite, Harley Davidson, Disney, and Yankee Candles.

- Hewlett-Packard was started in a garage in 1939. Today the garage is a private museum known as the "birthplace of Silicon Valley."
- Ten miles from the HP garage, Steve Wozniak created Apple's first computers in 1976.
- Bill Gates and Paul Allen started Microsoft in a garage, and Larry Page and Sergey Brin started Google in a garage in 1998.
- Disney's first film studio was started in a Los Angeles garage in 1923.

Youngest entrepreneurs. There are many examples of successful young entrepreneurs, some of whom launched a business before they were teenagers. Here's a sample of a few who may just become the next billion-dollar business owner:

- **Moziah "Mo" Bridges** – Mo launched Mo's Bows, a stylish handmade bow tie collection in 2011 at age nine. Two years later, he appeared on ABC's Shark Tank, and investor Daymond John became his mentor. In 2017, Mo signed a seven-figure licensing deal with the NBA to feature the NBA's logo on his apparel.
- **Ben Pasternak** – Australian tech-savvy Ben Pasternak developed his first app brain teaser game called "Impossible Rush" at age fifteen in 2014. The app peaked at number 16 on the US App Store (iOS) charts with millions of downloads. In 2018, he cofounded Simulate, a nutrition technology company featuring plant-based signature product NUGGS.
- **Ryan Kaji** – In 2015, Ryan's parents launched a YouTube channel featuring their three-year-old toy enthusiast son to review toys. Ryan's world (formerly Ryan ToysReview) is geared toward children aged two through six and has developed into a multi-million-dollar empire with billions of views.

- **Hart Main** – At age 13, Hart founded ManCan Candles, which are "manly" scented candles sold in soup cans to earn money to purchase a $1,200 bike. ManCan candles are sold in more than 150 stores, with nationwide sales exceeding six figures annually.
- **Jack Kim** – In 2011, social entrepreneur Jack Kim, age 15, launched Benelab, a nonprofit search engine founded "to make philanthropy easy and more accessible." The nonprofit operates on a crowdsourced model and donates all revenue to a unique charity every month.
- **Rachel Zietz** – Rachel launched Gladiator Lacrosse out of frustration with the quality of her lacrosse rebounder. She set out to develop a sturdier product to address this problem. The firm now has other products and exceeded $7 million in revenue in 2020, following the acquisition of All Ball Pro.
- **Willow Tufano** – The 14-year-old bought a house in Florida for $12,000 in 2012 as an investment. She renovated the house and then began renting it for $700/month.
- **Cameron Johnson** – Cameron began creating invitations at age nine, and two years later, he was making thousands of dollars selling cards through his company, Cheers and Tears.
- **Catherine Cook** – Catherine founded MyYearBook at age 15 with her brother Dave, age seventeen, in 2005. Based on the concept of a high school yearbook, the teen social networking site allows members to create profiles and interact with each other. Latino social media network Quepasa acquired the site for $100 million in 2011.
- **Ashley Qualls** – At age 14, Ashley launched whateverlife.com, conceived initially as a personal portfolio of her graphics and photos. It evolved to provide free Myspace layouts and tutorials for teens. In the first few months, she generated $70,000 in sales per month from her heavily trafficked site, primarily from advertising revenues.
- **Fraser Doherty** – Fraser started making jams from his grandmother's recipes in 2003 at age fourteen. By 2007, his company SuperJam had $750,000 in sales. He has also founded Envelope Coffee and is the cofounder of Beer52.
- **Josh Feinsilber** – Josh founded Gimkit, an app-based digital quiz gaming platform used by teachers to help students learn. The students are awarded in-game credits when they have learned and memorized different concepts. It is currently in use by schools in more than one 100 countries.
- **Hillary Yip** – Hillary is the CEO of Minor Mynas, which she founded at age 10 in 2016, making her one of the youngest CEOs worldwide. Minor Mynas is an online educational platform for children that facilitates language learning through live video calls and chat features.
- **Adora Svitak** – Adora is an author, speaker, and advocate for causes including feminism, youth empowerment, and literacy. Adora started writing when she was four and gave one hundred talks before age 13. Her 2010 TED talk "What Adults Can Learn From Kids" has 6.7 million views (February 2022).

Most successful women entrepreneurs. You'll definitely recognize these names:

- **Oprah Winfrey** – She grew up on an isolated farm in Mississippi and started a career in television. She is now a multi-billionaire philanthropist with her own TV network and magazine.
- **Beyoncé** – This top-selling solo artist has millions of dollars in endorsement deals and a $60 million contract with Netflix.
- **Tory Burch** – The founder of her namesake company, Tory Burch, has a $1 billion net worth.

Interesting entrepreneur ideas. No idea is too small — or too "out there." Consider these:
- WiFi Tea Kettle, which you can start and change settings for via your phone.
- Selfie Toaster, which makes toast with a picture of your face.
- Air umbrella, which pushes high bursts of air above you, so you don't get wet.
- A 3D-printed pancake maker.

85% of jobs that will exist in 2030 haven't been invented yet.
(Institute for the Future)

Youngest entrepreneur to appear on *Shark Tank*- Moziah Bridges of Mo's Bows.

33% of small businesses get started with less than $5,000.
(SBA)

Boss Up: Great High School-Based Business Ideas

Are you ready to be your own boss? Here are simple businesses that an entrepreneurial teen can start in high school. You may also help someone and make money along the way!

- Academic tutor
- Music/Art lessons
- Babysitting
- Computer setup/tech support
- Photographer/Videographer (for events, pets, etc.)
- Selling handmade goods/crafts retail or online (e.g., t-shirt designer)
- Reseller of products through Facebook Marketplace, eBay, or Etsy
- Farmer's market vendor handmade goods/beauty products or food items
- Social media influencer
- Errand-running (e.g., dry-cleaning, grocery shopping)

- Car washing
- Pet-sitting/dog-walking
- House-sitting
- Lawn care business/gardening
- Graphic/web designer
- Data entry
- Create an app or online game
- Party entertainment services (e.g., clown, magician, balloon artist)
- Snow/leaf removal
- Garage sale organizer
- Fitness trainer
- Translation services (if you're bilingual)

Exercise: Plan Your Brand!

Fill out this rubric to get a jump-start on your next entrepreneurial endeavor.

Social media can help broadcast the unique stories and adventures of you and your business. How can you utilize these platforms to share your mission, vision, and unique value?	Social and Professional Networks (Twitter, Facebook, Instagram, LinkedIn, TikTok, etc.)	Blogging and Microblogging (Tumblr, WordPress, etc.)	Personal Website (Google Sites, Wix.com, etc.)	Video-Sharing Sites (YouTube, Vimeo, etc.)
How is your competition currently utilizing these platforms?				
What aspects of your competitors' marketing strategy make sense for your business?				
What aspects of your competitors' marketing strategy do you not like and want to avoid or improve upon?				
How would you leverage what you have learned about your competition to develop your own unique social message?				
How will this content help your brand and business?				

Entrepreneurship Exercise: Becoming an Entrepreneur

Throughout this book, you have spent time learning about things you love, you excel at, and that can help you make an impact. Now it is time to use this knowledge to develop a big, bold business idea. Below, find a series of activities to assist you.

Similar to the scientific method you practiced in science class, many entrepreneurs try to identify and ultimately solve problems. Along the way, there is a testing of ideas, opportunities for failure to lead to innovation, the chance to make a difference, and plenty of hard work.

Simply put, entrepreneurs must identify problems and offer solutions that others are willing to buy. Being observant and curious are essential mindsets that allow us to ask questions that often require innovative solutions. Those who wander through life aimlessly may miss opportunities that those who are more aware of their surroundings see more easily.

For this first activity, think of places that you frequent. This place may be in your house, neighborhood, school, or even online. Use this table to document your observations.

Step 1: Planning

Location	Why did you choose to focus on this location?	What did you see that you liked?	What did you not like?	What entrepreneurial opportunities may exist?

Step 2: Which location will you focus on?
Include a picture of the place!

Step 3: What features/elements do you like most about this location?

A._____

B._____

C._____

D._____

E._____

Step 4: Describe a problem that you identified in this location.

Problem	
This is a problem because…	
This is a problem for people who…	

Step 5: Describe two potential entrepreneurial opportunities that would offer a solution to this problem.

Problem	
Entrepreneurial Opportunity 1 (Product or service):	
Entrepreneurial Opportunity 2 (Product or service):	

BRANDAMENTALS

And in the meantime, commit these top takeaways to memory:

1 **Teen entrepreneurship is on the rise.** Around the country, more and more teens are launching their own businesses. And some of them grow into corporate powerhouses.

2 **All entrepreneurs share a few top traits.** There are common characteristics to all entrepreneurs, like grit, passion, and creativity.

3 **Tap into the diverse set of entrepreneurship programs.** There is no shortage of programs that can give entrepreneurial teens a leg up. There are camps, clubs, membership organizations, and more.

4 **Don't reinvent the wheel.** You don't need a brand-new idea to be a teenage entrepreneur. Consider a business that leverages your existing skills, like tutoring, babysitting, or website development.

PART X — DOING GOOD

This section was a late addition to the book and was not included in my initial outline. But I realize that it may be the most important part of the book.

As I write, the world feels very broken. The new decade began with a presidential impeachment followed by a global pandemic. Then came George Floyd's death at the hands of Minneapolis police (among numerous other race-related injustices), which sparked protests and unrest worldwide. And Russia's invasion of Ukraine means the threat of World War III hovers over us. To put it concisely: Emotions are very raw. Like millions, I am filled with intense outrage, grief, and hopelessness. Many of us are crying out for meaningful change.

To face everything that's happening in the world, we must begin with a look in the mirror. Self-reflection also connects back to one of the most important exercises (Part 1) in this book: self-awareness.

Self-awareness about ethics, compassion, listening, kindness, gratitude, generosity, and so much more. For change to happen, we all need to "do good." In the words of Gandhi, "The best way to find yourself is to lose yourself in the service of others."

> *In today's world, empathy, tolerance and effective listening are all traits that we seek in future students.*
> *A student who sees value in interacting with people very different from themselves is a future graduate who will be able to adapt in today's complex world.*
>
> **— Jennifer Winge, VP for Enrollment, College of Wooster, Ohio**

An Expression of Empathy

The word that comes to mind these days is "empathy" — the ability to understand and be sensitive to others' feelings and perspectives. Empathy is at the heart of what it means to be human. It's a foundation for acting ethically and forging healthy relationships with family, friends, and business colleagues. Concern for others' feelings is a virtue that is sorely lacking today. Turn on CNN or scroll through social media posts, and you realize that we are suffering from an empathy deficit.

In my quest to learn more about empathy, I turned to Dr. Michele Borba, an internationally renowned educational psychologist and expert in parenting, bullying, and character development. She is also the author of *Unselfie: Why Empathetic Kids Succeed in Our All-About-Me World.*

Dr. Borba explains that "most people feel empathy is locked in the DNA. But empathy can be cultivated and is an ongoing process — you can even heighten it in middle age." She believes that empathy is perhaps the most essential twenty-first-century life skill, and it gives kids an advantage. Dr. Borba explains how research indicates that empathetic kids are more employable, social, kind, resilient, and collaborative. Alternatively, less empathetic children are less engaged, more aggressive, and less likely to get a good job after graduating from school.

Dr. Borba coined the phrase "Selfie Syndrome," which suggests that the force behind today's selfie culture — the belief that we are the center of the world — creates a decreased focus on others. This lack of empathy manifests itself in peer cruelty, bullying, cheating, a weaker capacity for moral reasoning, and a mental-health epidemic. It essentially hampers kids' ability to collaborate, innovate, and problem-solve — all necessary skills for a better society.

The good news? Dr. Borba shared four strategies teens can undertake to prioritize things like kindness, morality, and resiliency:

Practice kindness regularly. Tuning into others' feelings, perspectives, and circumstances takes practice. Develop a WE, not ME mindset. Practice teamwork and collaboration, and seek contact with individuals of different races, cultures, ages, genders, abilities, and beliefs in school, after school, or at summer camp.

Be a good digital citizen. Teens tend to spend a lot of time "looking down" while texting. Instead, be mindful and look up more. Face-to-face interactions are the best way to read emotions and develop empathy. The longer you are plugged in, the more likely you are to be narcissistic. Consider scheduling times to be digitally unplugged and then stick to them.

Use stories to develop moral imagination. Build your empathy muscle by reading books and watching movies, exploring the minds of diverse characters. On Dr. Borba's must-read list of empathy-building books are: *Black Like Me* by John Howard Griffin, *Great Expectations* by Charles Dickens, *Lord of the Flies* by William Golding, *Of Mice and Men* by John Steinbeck, *Pride* *and Prejudice* by Jane Austen, *The Color of Water* by James McBride, *The Diary of Anne Frank* by Anne Frank, *The Outsiders* by S.E. Hinton, and *To Kill a Mockingbird* by Harper Lee.

Find your inner hero. Be an upstander rather than a bystander. An example of this would be to diffuse a bullying situation. Moral courage is a special inner strength that motivates us to act on our empathic urges and helps others despite the consequences. It's not always easy. Sometimes, there are risks, and it may not rate as "cool" to other kids. But standing up for others with justice and compassion will make the world a better place.

Doing Good through Community Service

Let's face it: it's pretty much expected to have some type of community service on your résumé for college and your career. Before you choose your community service project, it's important to understand how colleges will evaluate these experiences. Harvard's Graduate School of Education joined together with a coalition of college admissions officers to publish a report in 2016 that includes recommendations related to community service:

- Choose community service projects **based on your interests and passions**.
- Spend **at least one year** on a sustained service project.
- Although individual projects are valuable, **community engagement projects** are encouraged. This means working in groups on a community project, like beautifying a local park.
- Work on community service projects that **deepen your understanding of diversity** — not by "doing for" people from different backgrounds, but by "doing with."
- Don't try to "game" community service with a set number of hours or impressive service in a faraway place. Focus on **building skills and generating ethical and emotional awareness.**

These recommendations are also fitting for employment. Rather than selecting extracurriculars that you (or your parents) believe will increase the odds of acceptance into your dream school, you need to find a community service project that YOU find personally meaningful. What matters most is that it comes from a heartfelt place.

I had the opportunity to interview many admission officers and educational consultants and found a common thread: They all value authenticity and transparency and want to see a sincere commitment to community involvement in the student's application. Volunteering isn't just a résumé-builder; the applicant must be prepared to explain why they have chosen their community service and what it means to them.

With so many charitable causes out there, it can be hard to choose just one. Whether your passion is working with animals, helping people with disabilities, supporting developing nations, or environmentalism, below are tips and resources to support your community service efforts.

Animal Shelters & Adoption Centers	Arts & Culture	Community Development
Education (Tutoring/Mentoring)	Environment/Conservation	Health
Human Services	International Research and Public Policy	Religion
Disaster Relief	Disability Support	Political & Advocacy Groups
Food Banks & Homeless Shelters	Trade & Professional Associations	

Your Community Service Checklist

Volunteering is a great way to give back to your community and make a difference in the lives of others. But it's not always easy to know where to start. So here is a checklist to ensure volunteering success:

Identify opportunities that match your passions and interests. Think strategically. What do you hope to gain from the experience? What causes are important to you? Do you want to work with animals, kids, or individuals with disabilities? Consider the goals, skills, knowledge, and unique talents you can bring to the organization. Narrow down your options by figuring out what excites and matters most to you. Finding a community service activity that matches your experience and passions will make you more engaged in the work. Do you want to devote your time locally or to a larger national effort? Do you prefer opportunities that are online or offline?

Find the right organization or cause. Once you identify the type of community service activity you are interested in, it's time to find an organization or cause that resonates with you. Research available volunteer opportunities, both online and offline. In many areas, there are also local nonprofit matchmakers — more on them soon. Reading reviews and speaking to those who have volunteered at a particular organization can inform your decision. You may also want to check out charity-rating organizations such as Charity Navigator, Guidestar, GreatNonprofits, and BBB Wise Giving Alliance before deciding where to invest your time.

Understand your responsibilities for the position. Each organization will have specific requirements and expectations for volunteers, so it's essential to understand what's expected of you before committing. Community service tasks can range from teaching kids how to read to walking dogs to stuffing envelopes. Each volunteer brings a unique mix of skills and interests to the table. Apply if you believe the responsibilities of the position are right for you.

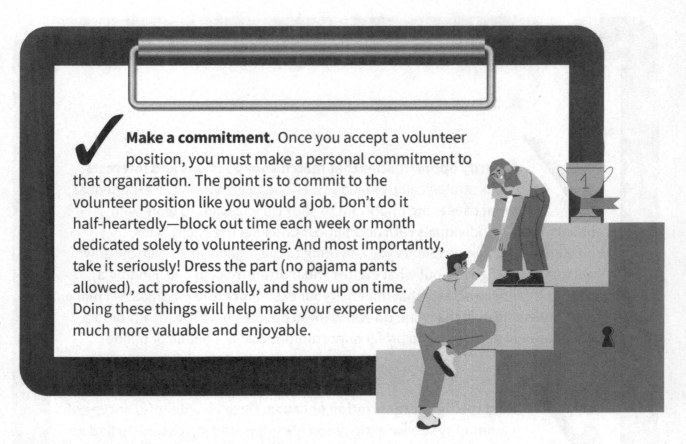

✓ **Make a commitment.** Once you accept a volunteer position, you must make a personal commitment to that organization. The point is to commit to the volunteer position like you would a job. Don't do it half-heartedly—block out time each week or month dedicated solely to volunteering. And most importantly, take it seriously! Dress the part (no pajama pants allowed), act professionally, and show up on time. Doing these things will help make your experience much more valuable and enjoyable.

"Do Good" Resources

Below is a sampling of community service resources. (Note: Some organizations require volunteers to be 18 years or older.)

Whether you want to tackle climate change or food insecurity, take the time to find the right opportunity. Searching for volunteer opportunities has never been easier. Use these websites to search and contact nonprofits for volunteer opportunities. Many online resources allow you to search for volunteer opportunities by location (city, zip code) and interest. Then, you can send a message directly from the website to the volunteer coordinator or organization. Check out these websites below to find your perfect match:

Volunteer Directly

Do Something   **www.DoSomething.org**

Do Something is the largest nonprofit volunteer organization exclusively for young people and social change to help solve real-world problems. DoSomething has activated five million young people (and counting!) to bring about social change and participate in civic action campaigns to make an impact on causes they care about. Causes include ending gun violence, addressing hate speech, improving child literacy, and more. One of DoSomething's most widely recognized projects was members successfully urging Apple to diversify their emojis. Members can also earn scholarships through community service. **Free for volunteers.**

SignUpGenius   www.signupgenius.com

SignUpGenius.com is a site to sign up for groups and volunteer management. They have an impressive list of fifty community service ideas for teen volunteers that help teens determine the service opportunities that reflect their passion. Browse this list for ideas based on interests, time, and talent. No fees are required to use the site and sign up for events. **A fee-based subscription provides enhanced tools for organizing and monitoring events.**

Junior Achievement USA   www.jausa.ja.org

Junior Achievement (JA) enables its members to help students with schoolwork and life skills in their community. The volunteering section describes the training curriculum and lists volunteer activities. Volunteer commitments range from a single school day to a weekly one-hour visit for five to ten weeks. **Free to volunteers.**

United Way   www.unitedway.org

Established in 1887, United Way is one of the oldest and most esteemed volunteer organizations. There are many ways to get involved in United Way projects locally. Using the volunteer search tool, you can browse opportunities by keyword and location. Volunteers can then filter by skill, category, and activity type to find a fitting project. In addition, the Student United Way program will help you organize your peers to tackle pressing social problems in your community. **Free for volunteers.**

Random Acts of Kindness   www.randomactsofkindness.org

Random Acts of Kindness is a website for inspiration. It features ideas on how to be kind to each other and your community at school, at home, and at work. Inspirational resources include kindness quotes, a blog, videos, and stories. **Free to volunteers.**

Aggregators of Volunteer Opportunities
(Match volunteers with organizations in need)

TeensGive   www.teensgive.org

Founded by two high school students, TeensGive is a nonprofit organization designed to provide service opportunities for high school students seeking rewarding volunteer opportunities that align with their skills. Teens can tutor in person or virtually using the organization's curriculum tools. Students interested in starting a TeensGive chapter at their school must adhere to the organization's guidelines. Students can also teach an entrepreneurship curriculum called Counting Cupcakes if so inclined. **Free to volunteers.**

Interns 4-Good   www.interns4good.org

The site connects high school students with virtual, skill-based internship opportunities at nonprofit organizations to develop professional skills while giving back to worthy causes. Select an internship that fits your schedule and matches your interest and skills. Opportunities range from research to supporting a nonprofit's finance department to graphic design, website/app design, and writing. **Registration is free.**

Lion's Heart   www.lionsheartservice.org

Lion's Heart is an organization that curates teen volunteering opportunities from national nonprofits like the American Red Cross, ASPCA, Make-A-Wish Foundation, Toys for Tots, and local nonprofits. Volunteer opportunities are available to teens either as a group or individually. You will also be able to showcase your achievements via a digital portfolio and participate in awards such as the President's Volunteer Service Award, the Congressional Award, and other honors. Lion's Heart also curates college scholarship opportunities for its members. **There are annual dues and a one-time enrollment fee.**

VolunteerMatch   www.volunteermatch.org

Established in 1998, Volunteer Match is one of the largest databases connecting nonprofits with volunteers. Since its inception, VolunteerMatch has connected more than 15 million volunteers to organizations globally. Volunteer opportunities are available in over 25 categories, from education, homelessness, and the environment to disaster relief, hunger, and animals. **Free to volunteers.**

Idealist   www.idealist.org

Idealist provides volunteer opportunities, internships, and job listings. Volunteer+ is a tool that aggregates volunteerism and other action opportunities in the nonprofit sector, pulling from sites around the web to provide a comprehensive database of volunteer opportunities from around the world. You can search organizations by keyword and location, helping you find a local nonprofit that may need help, even if there isn't a volunteer role listed. Idealist also has mutual aid groups, idealist days (monthly days of action), and a social network for good on iOS. **Free to volunteers.**

Engage Points of Light   **www.engage.pointsoflight.org**

Formerly known as All For Good, Engage is Points of Light's platform for volunteers seeking ways to help in their communities and to find opportunities and organizations that need their time, talents, and passion. Individuals can search for volunteer projects, nonprofits can post and manage event sign-ups, and visitors are invited to start projects of their own. Filters allow you to customize your volunteerism, choosing in-person or remote, an ongoing time commitment vs. limited time, location, and issue area. You can connect to various opportunities, from a local animal shelter to an overseas charity. **The site is free to volunteers over age 13, although some opportunities have age restrictions.**

JustServe   **www.justserve.org**

JustServe helps people find volunteer opportunities in their local community using filters for desired location, group vs. individual, skill set, and categories of interest. Potential volunteers can browse through past success stories, which showcase events and activities. Volunteers must be sixteen or older. **Free for volunteers.**

AmeriCorps   **www.americorps.gov**

AmeriCorps is a federal agency that offers short- and long-term volunteer gigs and opportunities to get involved locally in daily, weekly, or monthly events. Their Find an Opportunity page allows volunteers to look for events and organizations in their local area. Students can also filter for opportunities appropriate for their age. So whether you want to build houses, provide meals to those in need, or support youth literacy, there are many ways you can make a difference through AmeriCorps. Open to all ages. **Free to participate.**

GozAround   **www.gozaround.com**

GozAround prides itself on volunteers making a difference in their unique way, whether it's through a virtual volunteer role or offsetting your carbon footprint. Volunteers can register and input their skills and preferences based on their interests, skills, schedules, and location. GozAround also adds a fun gratification element, allowing volunteers to set goals for their hours and track their giving progress. The GozAround network also promotes sharing through social channels. **Free for volunteers.**

Volunteer.gov   **www.volunteer.gov**

The website is filled with opportunities for volunteers interested in nature, conservation, and animal protection. The website allows volunteers to search for roles by state, project, or date. Whether serving as a campground host, translating Spanish for park rangers, or helping at therapeutic gardens, there are many ways to get outdoors and give back. No experience is necessary. **Free for volunteers.**

GivePulse   **www.givepulse.com**

GivePulse is a search tool that lets you search for local events, groups, and causes you care most about and register for events from your dashboard. From the GivePulse search page, you can filter by Sustainable Development Goals (SDGs), causes, skills, and other criteria to refine your search. GivePulse helpers can also track their hours and donations on the website. Volunteers can collaborate with friends, family members, and partners on GivePulse projects to make an even more significant impact. **Free for volunteers.**

Voluntourism Organizations

Global Volunteers
Website: globalvolunteers.og/

Global Volunteers provides volunteer opportunities for students, families, professionals, and retirees. Opportunities last from one to three weeks, immersing volunteers deep in the culture of those they're supporting. Projects include teaching English, supporting women's crafts cooperatives, improving computer literacy, and educating people on nutrition. From Cuba to China, there's something for everyone. A parent or legal guardian must accompany minors. **Program costs vary by location/duration.**

Globe Aware   **www.globeaware.org**

Volunteers can make an impact in destinations like Thailand, Costa Rica, and Peru. Globe Aware offers many volunteer opportunities for families, retirees, solo travelers, and university groups. Globe Aware is committed to providing programs where volunteers give back and develop cultural awareness. Globe Aware combines beautiful and enriching destinations with meaningful volunteer opportunities. A parent or legal guardian must accompany minors. **Program costs vary by location/duration.**

International Volunteer HQ   **www.volunteerhq.org**

International Volunteer HQ connects people with opportunities abroad. The program spans 40 countries and includes projects that target nearly every interest imaginable with specific programs for teens. A few project areas include sea turtle and marine conservation, teaching, arts and music, sports, and women's empowerment. There are opportunities throughout Europe, North America, South America, Africa, Asia, the Middle East, and the Pacific. A designated guardian must accompany teens under the age of sixteen, and 16- and 17-year-olds can participate with parental consent. **Program fees vary based on the destination and duration of the program.**

Whether you want to tackle climate change or food insecurity, invest the time to find the right opportunity. Searching for volunteer opportunities has truly never been easier. Many of the resources listed above allow volunteers to search for opportunities by location (city, zip code) and interest and also allow you to directly message the volunteer coordinator or organization. While there's nothing better than having a live volunteer experience, don't rule out online opportunities, which also allow you to contribute in a meaningful way.

Circling back:
Remember that empathy is at the basis of all healthy personal and business relationships and is essential to your overall well-being. Additionally, by "doing good," you will gain new skills, such as time management, interpersonal, leadership, and problem-solving skills for future success.

In summary:
Reaching out to others in need should be a way of life, not an infrequent thing. I can't think of a better way to end this book as you begin your journey to greatness.

BRANDAMENTALS

And in the meantime, commit these top takeaways to memory:

1 **Empathy should always be a top priority…** The ability to understand and be sensitive to others' feelings and perspectives is key to being successful — and fulfilled — in life.

2 **…and is a skill you can develop**. Empathy is not a virtue you either have or don't. By making things like kindness and moral imagination regular habits, you can grow your capacity for empathy.

3 **Community service is essential.** College admissions officers and hiring managers expect to see volunteering on your résumé. But that's not the only reason to give back: It's also incredibly fulfilling.

4 **There are countless resources to kick off your volunteer journey.** There is no shortage of nonprofits and causes that need your help. Further, there are organizations specifically designed to match you with volunteer opportunities based on your interests.

WRAP UP

You may have reached the end of this book, but your personal brand journey is just beginning. That's because a strong personal brand is never static: it's constantly adapting and improving. You will add new chapters throughout your academic and professional career. And while some chapters will reveal surprising new dimensions that revise people's understanding of who you are, ideally, they should reinforce your brand's core values.

It won't always be easy. Unfortunate events happen even to the best of brands — like sending a tweet that could be misinterpreted or publishing an unprofessional photo. You may have reputational damage to live down at some point, and that will be a test of your brand-management skills.

Each individual's brand is unique, from teens to retirees, but the process of uncovering, cultivating, and growing a brand is universal. You now have new inspirations and tools to get out there, imagine, and create.

RESOURCE LIST

Career Research

MY NEXT MOVE https://www.mynextmove.org/,
an interactive tool for job seekers and students to learn about tasks and
skills, salary information, and more for over nine hundred different careers.

Career Tests For High School Students

The career assessment tests below evaluate your skills, interests, and personality type to help
you choose the right career path for you.

Holland Code (RIASEC) Test   www. openpsychometrics.org/tests/RIASEC/
This free test has 48 questions. It matches users against six types of career interest categories.
The results page explains the user's career interest category and provides information on
suitable careers.

Naviance   www. powerschool.com
Naviance is a college, career, and life readiness (CCLR) platform that helps middle and high
school students discover their strengths, explore college and career interests, create actionable
goals, and find their best-fit path after high school. Trusted by more than 13,000 schools and
more than 10 million students, this robust solution promotes college and career readiness by
encouraging academic rigor and aligning student strengths and interests to long-term goals.

The MAPP. (Motivational Appraisal Personal Potential)   www.assessment.com
This free, 22-minute career assessment is geared toward students, graduates, and working
adults. More than 8 million people in nearly every country in the world have taken the MAPP
test since its inception in 1995.

Princeton Review Career Quiz   www.princetonreview.com/quiz/career-quiz
This free, 24-question job quiz by the test-prep company The Princeton Review is on the shorter
side for career aptitude tests but gives detailed results and job advice.

CareerExplorer   www.careerexplorer.com/career-test

Uses advanced machine learning, psychometrics, and career satisfaction data to make recommendations.

CareerOneStop Interest Assessment
www.careeronestop.org/ExploreCareers/Assessments/interests.aspx

A five-minute, 30-question career quiz from the US Department of Labor will help students figure out possible career choices. It ranks your interest in fifteen broad categories. Should the test result indicate you have a high interest in art and technology, for example, you can consider a career that combines the two, e.g., video game design or graphic design.

TruityCareer Assessment   www.truity.com

A free career personality test using Myers and Briggs' theory of personality types combined with the Holland Code system of career typing provides a report matching personality, strengths, and aptitude to determine your ideal career.

Scholarship/Contests/Awards/ Leadership Opportunities

STEM (Science, Technology, Engineering, Math)

STEM Leadership Center   www.stemedcenter.org

The STEM Leadership Center is a 501(c)(3) formed by master science educators to design engaging science experiences for students and NGSS-based professional development for teachers. The center specializes in developing project-based STEM curricula and methods of instruction that effectively integrate technology and engineering design into classroom instruction.

Davidson Fellows   www.davidsongifted.org/gifted-programs/fellows-scholarship

Recognized by Forbes as "one of the nation's most prestigious undergraduate scholarships," the Davidson Fellows scholarship was named one of "the 10 Biggest Scholarships in the World" by TheBestColleges.org and one of the "7 Prestigious Undergrad Scholarships" in U.S. News & World Report.

ExploraVision   **www.exploravision.org/**

The ExploraVision competition for K–12 students engages students in real-world problem-solving with a strong emphasis on STEM ExploraVision challenges students to envision and communicate new technology ten or more years in the future through collaborative brainstorming and research. Teachers lead their students in groups of two to four to simulate research and development. Past winners have envisioned technologies ranging from a hand-held food allergen detector to a new device to help people who have lost limbs regain movement in real time.

Modeling the Future Challenge
www.competitionsciences.org/competitions/2021-22-modeling-the-future-challenge

This real-world competition for high school students combines math modeling, data analysis, and risk management. Students conduct their own research projects modeling real-world data to analyze risks and make recommendations to companies, industry groups, governments, or organizations. This challenge tasks students to use critical thinking, mathematical reasoning, and analytical skills to help guide future decisions based on their risk analysis. Students also have a shot at a part of the $60,000 purse.

Future Problem Solving Program International
www.competitionsciences.org/competitions/future-problem-solving-program

Founded in 1974 by creativity pioneer Dr. E. Paul Torrance, Future Problem Solving Program International (FPSPI) stimulates critical and creative thinking skills. It also encourages students to develop a vision for the future and prepares students for leadership roles. In addition, FPSPI engages students in creative problem-solving within the curriculum and provides competitive opportunities. FPSPI involves thousands of students annually from around the world.

Solve For Tomorrow   **www.competitionsciences.org/competitions/solve-for-tomorrow**

The Samsung Solve for Tomorrow competition invites teachers to lead a group of students in creating a STEM-centered solution that addresses a need in their communities. As teams are selected to move through each phase, they must provide more project details and are awarded prizes of increasing value. Teachers and students compete to win a share of $2 million for their schools. The National Winner prize is $100,000 in technology and classroom materials.

For more SCHOLARSHIPS, CONTESTS & AWARDS examples, please visit the Institute of Competition Sciences **www.competitionsciences.org/**.

Business/Entrepreneurship

Conrad Spirit of Innovation Challenge   www.conradchallenge.org

The Conrad Challenge is a purpose-driven innovation competition creating the next generation of entrepreneurs. Students between the ages of 13 through 18 are eligible to participate. With the challenge's step-by-step guidance and the support of industry experts, students can expand their collaboration, creativity, critical thinking, and communication skills.

W.I.S.E. Award   www.nmoe.org/student-ideas-better-americatm

Enter an idea for a new product or improvement for an existing product or procedure. Monetary prizes are awarded each month. This is an ongoing contest, and there is no deadline.

National Youth Entrepreneur of the Year Contest
www. lemonadeday.org/YEOYcontest-rules

The Lemonade Day® national Youth Entrepreneur Award (the "Contest") is a competition in which entrants submit their Business Results via prepaid postcard, online via Lemonade Day city or national website, or paper form submission to the local City program Director.

National Gallery for America's Young Inventors   www.nmoe.org

The National Gallery for America's Young Inventors is a museum of young American inventors whose ideas hold promise to positively impact our society. Its purpose is to preserve and promote great inventions produced by America's youth. The National Gallery inducts up to six young people in grades K-12 annually.

Unilever Young Entrepreneurs Award
www.oneyoungworld.com/unilever-young-entrepreneurs-awards

Unilever's competition is for those who have an initiative, product, or service already in action tackling a sustainability problem. Entrepreneurs ages 18–35 from around the world are eligible to enter. Initiatives must have already progressed beyond the idea stage and started making an impact.

Youth Biz Stars   www. yacenter.org/youthbiz/stars-business-competition

Young American's Center for Financial Education hosts the Youth Biz Stars competition each year. Youth business owners at all stages in the game are welcome to apply. They could win up to $5,000, plus mentorship with a leading business owner in the community.

The Conrad Foundation's Conrad Challenge   **www.conradchallenge.org**
The Conrad Challenge is a purpose-driven innovation competition for students aged 13–18. Students apply science, technology and innovation to solve problems with global impact.

Liberal Arts

This category includes but is not limited to students interested in pursuing English, History, Philosophy, Communications, Foreign Languages.

National Society of High School Scholars (NSHSS) Creative Writing Scholarship
www.nshss.org/scholarships/s/nshss-creative-writing-scholarship/
High school students of all ages are eligible for this creative writing scholarship, sponsored by NSHSS. Students can submit work (that has not been previously published) in one or both categories: poetry and fiction. In the poetry category, students may submit their original poetry in any style (formal verse, free verse, or experimental). In the fiction category, students may submit a piece of short fiction (5,000 words limit) and can choose any genre, including graphic novel or short story. A prize of $2,000 will be awarded to three student winners in each category.

LITA/Christian Larew Memorial Scholarship In Library And Information Technology
www.unigo.com/scholarships/by-major/english-scholarships/litachristian-larew-memorial-scholarship-in-library-and-information-technology
Graduate students who have completed no more than 12 hours in an approved master of library science (MLS) program while attending an ALA-accredited school are eligible for this award. In addition, eligible students must plan to follow a career in the library and information technology field.

US Institute of Peace National Peace Essay Contest
www.usip.org/public-education/students/AFSAEssayContest

USIP partners with the American Foreign Service Association (AFSA) on the annual National High School Essay Contest. The yearly contest engages high school students in learning and writing about peace and conflict issues, encouraging appreciation for diplomacy's role in building partnerships that can advance peacebuilding and protect national security.

International Philosophy Olympiad (IPO)   **www.philosophy-olympiad.org**

The IPO is a competition for high-school students. It was established in 1993 by an initiative of the Department of Philosophy of Sofia University to invite a group of philosophers from various countries.

National WWII Museum Essay Contest   **www.nationalww2museum.org/**

The National WWII Museum in New Orleans offers a first prize of $1,000 to high school students who write compelling and historically interesting responses to prompts involving World War II history. The winning essays are published on the website and receive national recognition.

Chinese Bridge
**www. confucius.aueb.gr/en/competitions/chinese-bridge-competition/
national-chinese-bridge-competition**

Chinese Bridge is an international competition for second language learners held annually for high school and college students. Since its 2002 launch, more than one thousand college student contestants from 80 countries have participated in the semifinals and finals in China.

ABOUT THE AUTHORS

Stacey Ross Cohen: In the world of branding, few experts possess the savvy and instinct of Stacey Cohen. An award-winning brand professional who earned her stripes on Madison Avenue and at major television networks before launching her own agency, Stacey specializes in finding, cultivating, and perfecting brands. She is the CEO and founder of Co-Communications, a public relations, marketing, and design agency with offices in New York and Connecticut. Since 1998, Stacey has coached individuals and businesses across various industries — from real estate and health care to education and professional services — and expertly positions their narratives in fiercely competitive markets. A staple at industry conferences, Stacey recently made her debut on the TEDx stage. She is a contributor at the *Huffington Post* and *Entrepreneur* and has been featured in *Forbes, Crain's, Entrepreneur,* and a suite of other national media. She holds a BS from Syracuse University, an MBA from Fordham University, and has a certificate from NYU Leonard Stern School of Business in Media, Technology, and Entertainment.

Stacey is an entrepreneur at heart: She started her first business when she was just 14 years old and is now a member of a prominent angel investor group. Standing out has always been a matter of course for her. As a twin, Stacey's struggle to cultivate her own identity made her more sensitive to the need to develop uniqueness. The book draws on Stacey's over 25 years of experience building both personal and business brands. She is extremely passionate about helping high school students cultivate, perfect, and activate their personal brands to become tomorrow's leaders. She believes that digital savvy is a learned skill and should be part of high school curricula.

Jason Shaffer: Jason Shaffer is a trailblazer in creating a progressive curriculum that equips and empowers middle and high school students with the necessary skills in today's innovation economy. Jason is currently an Innovation Institute instructor at Lake Highland Preparatory School, where he teaches entrepreneurship to middle school students to fuel work/life success. He previously developed the Personal Branding and Digital Communications curriculum for North Broward Preparatory School and has taught hundreds of students how to expertly manage their social media profiles and behaviors. Jason's curriculum, which was a graduation requirement at North Broward Prep, has become a model for schools nationwide. Jason has been recognized for his teaching excellence with North Broward's Soaring Eagle award and the Meritas Excellence in Teaching award. Jason received his BA in History from Florida Atlantic University.

Alan Katzman: Alan is a pioneer in developing and advancing techniques to teach students how to use social media. He helps teens build a compelling and reflective digital presence as a game-changing tool for creating academic and career success. Alan is a sought-after speaker for high school students, parents, and educational professionals while frequently participating in education-related events nationwide. Alan has been featured in The *New York Times, The Wall Street Journal, CNN, ABC News, NPR, USA Today, Forbes, Business Insider, and Social Media Today.* Alan made his foray into social media education with the launch of Social Assurity in 2013 and has licensed its social media courseware to thousands of students nationwide. Before forming Social Assurity, Alan served as executive legal counsel for several start-up and Fortune 500 technology companies, where he managed the law, compliance, and administrative functions. Alan received his BA from the University at Albany and his JD from Albany Law School.